PASS IT ON

A Bible Commentary for Laymen
First and Second Timothy

BY ROBERT H. MOUNCE

Regal
Books

A Division of GL Publications
Ventura, California, U.S.A.

© Copyright 1979 by GL Publications. All rights reserved.

Published by Regal Books
A Division of GL Publications
Ventura, California 93006
Printed in U.S.A.

Third Printing, 1984

Library of Congress Catalog Card No. 78-68851
ISBN 0-8307-0656-9

CONTENTS

A Teacher's Manual and Student Discovery Guide for use with *Pass It On* are available from your church supplier.

PREFACE

Pass It On (see 2 Tim. 2:2) is a layman's commentary on two letters written by the apostle Paul to his young friend and colleague Timothy. Its major goal is to clarify and explain the content of this first-century correspondence.

Paul lived a long time ago. The world he knew was halfway around the globe from modern America and separated in time by almost two thousand years. Yet what he had to say is highly relevant for us today. The love of money, for example, is still the root of all kinds of evil.

The primary role of a biblical expositor is to bring the meaning of the text into as sharp a focus as possible. This calls for a thorough knowledge of first-century culture and the willingness to understand a passage in its original setting before showing how it may speak to contemporary man.

I have found that when we understand clearly *what* Scripture is saying we have little trouble in knowing *how* it applies to our life. To rush into application before we grasp what it is that is to be applied is to run the risk of distorting God's Word and ending up with psychological insights rather than a "word from the beyond."

At the close of each section I have added a paragraph or two designed to encourage reflection on some major truth just discussed. These sections are printed in an alternate type style for easy recognition. If you agree that the ultimate goal of all Bible study is "love, which comes from a pure heart" (1 Tim. 1:5) you will want to take time and give special personal attention to these sections.

I have used the *New International Version* of the Bible as my basic text. As one of the best committee translations of the twentieth century it may well become the standard Bible of evangelical Christianity. The reader is encouraged to refer constantly to the text of Scripture while studying the commentary.

I have also quite often quoted from other Bible translations. These are listed in the front of this book.

My most sincere thanks go to Mary Ann McGehee who transformed a not too legible handwritten manuscript into a highly professional typescript.

R. Mounce

Robert H. Mounce

INTRODUCTION

The two letters to Timothy (along with the letter to Titus), normally called the pastoral epistles, are the last letters written by the apostle Paul. Since the historical data which they supply cannot be fitted into the life and ministry of Paul as we have it in Acts, it appears that they were written after Paul's release from the Roman imprisonment described in the last chapter of Acts.

First Timothy was written from Macedonia somewhere around the mid-sixties. Paul had left his young companion in Ephesus to take charge of the church. Concern for Timothy and for the congregation caused Paul to write what is often described as a "manual of church discipline." The presence of false teachers in Ephesus (whose consuming interest was idle speculation and irrelevant trivia) called for Timothy to assume his leadership role in a more dominant manner.

Paul wrote 2 Timothy from a prison in Rome. No more than a year or so had elapsed since his earlier letter. A note of loneliness runs through the apostle's final letter. It appears that he had already gone through a preliminary hearing in which no one except Luke stood by him. Recognizing that the "time of his departure" is at hand, Paul is anxious that Timothy, his dear son in the faith, come as quickly as possible.

For a more complete presentation of the background of 1 and 2 Timothy see the introductory section of Donald Guthrie's commentary, *The Pastoral Epistles*[1] or chapter 12 in Everett Harrison's *Introduction to the New Testament*.[2] Both volumes will supply additional bibliography.

Notes

1. Donald Guthrie, *The Pastoral Epistles*, Tyndale Bible Commentary (Grand Rapids: Wm. B. Eerdmans Publishing Co., 1957), pp. 11-53.
2. Everett F. Harrison, *Introduction to the New Testament* (Grand Rapids: Wm. B. Eerdmans Publishing Co., 1964), pp. 326-343.

PART 1
THE FIRST EPISTLE TO TIMOTHY

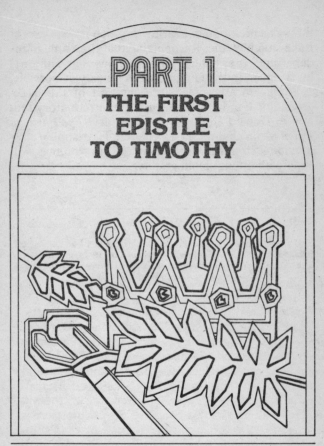

You will remember that the young convert, Timothy, joined Paul on his second missionary journey (see Acts 16:1-4) and labored faithfully by his side for the next 15 years or so. Recently Paul had left Timothy at Ephesus and now writes back by way of instruction and encouragement.

1

FIRST TIMOTHY ONE

Greetings (1:1,2)

Ancient letters never left you in doubt about who was doing the writing. They put it right out front. From—To—Greetings!

So the letter to Timothy begins, "Paul, an apostle of Christ Jesus." The instructions that follow are not to be taken as coming from someone who is no more than an elderly well-intentioned friend. They come from an apostle—one specifically commissioned and sent out from God (that is what the word means). Normally Paul says that his apostleship is "by the will of God" (2 Cor. 1:1), but here the expression is stronger. He has been made an apostle by the "command" of God (the term is often used of royal commands which must be obeyed absolutely).

The close relationship between Paul and Timothy is mirrored in Paul's reference to Timothy as "my true son in the faith." As used here "true" may mean trueborn (that is, a legitimate son of his father) or, and this is more probable, true in the sense of genuine or reliable. Timothy has faithfully carried out his responsibilities as a trustworthy disciple. As a result a close and intimate relationship has grown up between the old gospel warrior and his young lieutenant. Timothy is Paul's son in the faith.

Some have complained that the pastoral epistles are not especially theological. While it is true that they were written for practical purposes it does not follow that they are devoid of "theology." Even the opening salutation has a significant amount of compressed theology. God, for example, is designated not only as Father but also as Saviour. Outside these epistles this is said of God only twice in the New Testament. To the Jewish reader it would recall such Old Testament verses as Psalm 25:5, "Lead me in thy truth, and teach me, for thou art the God of my salvation" *(RSV)*. To the Greek reader, however, it may have suggested a contrast with the current pagan practice of referring to the emperor as Saviour. To both, portraying God as Saviour would serve as a reminder that God is in the business of delivering man from the guilt and power of sin.

The salutation also has a theology of the Son. Jesus is the hope of all believers. God as Saviour works through the incarnation, death, and resurrection of Christ the Son. The very name, Jesus, was given because "he will save his people from their sins" (Matt. 1:21). Thus, He is our hope.

But Jesus is also "our Lord." He is absolute master over the church. His commands are the marching orders of the church militant. Disobedience is treason.

Paul greets his companion with a triad of spiritual blessings. Grace (unmerited favor) is a Christian variation of the normal Greek salutation. Peace (well-being in the widest sense of the word) corresponds to the Hebrew greeting, *shalom*. To these

10

customary two Paul adds "mercy." Both grace and compassion are necessary for that state of inner well-being and wholeness which is to characterize the child of God.

Paul was an apostle of Christ Jesus. This means that he was *sent* on a mission for the Lord. He was an ambassador with a specific duty to carry out.

In what sense can it be said that we who live in the twentieth century are also apostles? Does 2 Corinthians 5:20 indicate that every believer is an apostle? As an apostle how faithfully have you carried out your divine commission?

How to Go Wrong (1:3-7)

Have you ever noticed how easy it is for a person to get all mixed up? No wonder they say that to err is human. The early church was no exception. They too had their "heretics." While most were not wild-eyed radicals, they nevertheless tended to absorb pagan ideas whose implications spelled trouble for the believing congregation.

Ephesus had its would-be teachers. They receive a good deal of attention in Paul's first letter to Timothy. They are discussed not only in the immediate paragraph but in 1:19,20; 4:2,3,7; and 6:2b-5,20,21 as well. We will be learning a lot about them as we proceed through the letter. For the moment they will serve to illustrate rather clearly "How to Go Wrong."

The first major step in going wrong is to *deviate from the apostolic teaching.* Paul urges Timothy to remain in Ephesus in order to "command certain men [apparently they were well known] not to teach false doctrines any longer" (v. 3). God's Word through the apostles is the unchanging basis for New Testament doctrine. In an earlier letter Paul was so upset by anyone who would preach a "different gospel" that he twice declared, "Let him be eternally condemned" (Gal. 1:8,9).

The second step is to *occupy yourself with a lot of sophisticated tomfoolery* that has little or nothing to do with the way believers are to live. Timothy is to warn the amateur philosophers about wasting their time and energy on "myths and endless genealogies." Commentators differ as to what these two terms represent. Apparently the ancients loved to speculate about the origins of their famous cities and developed elaborate genealogies for their prominent families. Alexander the Great, for example, constructed a lineage that went all the way back to the gods of Greek mythology.

Other commentators link the terms with an early philosophy known an gnosticism. They seem to describe the series of emanations which were said to link God (spirit and therefore good) with the world (material and therefore evil). Still others suggest a Jewish background with the terms reflecting the practice of allegorizing the Old Testament. Whatever the immediate background, it is clear that the problem was one of people wasting their time on trivial and speculative concerns.

The Christian faith is essentially a way of life. While it has a theology, this theology is never an end in itself. It is the explication of what God has done in Christ for the salvation of man. It is the basis and rationale for a transformed life. As faith apart from works is dead (see Jas. 2:26), theology apart from ethical change is worthless. Myths and endless genealogies may excite the intellect but they will never change the man.

A third way to go wrong is to *give up the "divine training that is in faith"* (v. 4, *RSV*), or, as the *Twen-*

tieth Century New Testament has it, "which is revealed in the Faith." Faith has its discipline. It requires the believer to live in a certain way. This we often forget.

Paul summarizes this way of life as "love that issues from a pure heart and a good conscience and sincere faith" (v. 5, *RSV*). Love is not romantic enchantment but a commitment of the will to place the welfare of others as a first priority. Calvary is the ultimate expression of what it means to love. God so loved that He *gave*.

Paul is concerned that the church at Ephesus grow in love, not in the ability to speculate endlessly about things that don't matter. It would appear from a letter written to the same church some 30 years later that they failed to get the message. Through John, the glorified Christ writes, "Yet I hold this against you: You have forsaken your first love" (Rev. 2:4).

For love to be genuinely Christian it must flow from a "pure heart," that is, without the intention of any personal gain. It must also issue from a "good conscience." The Greek word carries the idea of self-judgment. To act in good conscience means to have examined all the evidence—especially that which no one else can know—and proceed without hesitation or lingering doubts. "Sincere faith," the third member of this ethical triad, is open and honest trust without a shadow of pretense or hypocrisy.

It is by swerving from these basic requirements that some at Ephesus had wandered into vain discussion. Note that doctrinal deviation is not the cause but the result of ethical failure. It was *after* they had given up "divine training" (doing the things that faith requires) that they went "astray into a wilderness of words" *(NEB)*. Had they maintained the rigorous schedule of true faith they would never have wan-

13

dered off into the wastelands of vain discussion and useless speculation.

A final way to go wrong is to *desire a gift you obviously do not have.* Those at Ephesus "want to be teachers of the law, but they do not know what they are talking about or what they so confidently affirm" (v. 7). In New Testament times it was an honorable profession to be a teacher of the law. Gamaliel was one such teacher and Luke wrote that he was "honored by all the people" (Acts 5:34).

The Ephesian heretics desired the honor of posing as teachers. Unfortunately, they were ill-equipped for the task. Their confident assertions about the law revealed that not only were they ignorant of the subjects they propounded but they didn't even grasp the meaning of the words they were using. The church has always had its share of self-appointed intellectuals who seemingly take delight in confusing the clear teeachng of Scripture by insisting on philosophical subtleties that simply do not exist. James wisely counseled, "Not many of you should presume to be teachers, . . . because you know that we who teach will be judged more strictly" (Jas. 3:1). The advice would have fallen on deaf ears at Ephesus. One of the penalties of ignorance is the inability to recognize it.

It is painfully clear from this passage that the purpose of the Christian faith is to alter the way we live, not to provide us with philosophical trivia for endless argument.

Have you ever noticed how much easier it is to discuss issues such as the state of the heathen or the doctrine of election than it is to share with one another how God is shaping our lives to be more like Christ? Why do you suppose we so quickly veer off into nonessentials when it would be far more profitable to share our problems and pray for one another? If Satan attacks us at this point what does it say about the importance of faith as it relates to the way we live?

Law and Gospel (1:8-11)

After putting down the would-be teachers of the law for not understanding what they are talking about, Paul takes a moment to place law and gospel in proper perspective. "The law is good," he says, "if a man uses it properly." The basic purpose of the law is to restrain wickedness. It is okay to use it in this way. But the church is not under law. It exists within the freedom of the gospel. To put believers back under the law—and this is exactly what the false teachers were trying to do (note 4:2,3, "liars ... [who] forbid people to marry and order them to abstain from certain foods")—is to use the law illegally. Law is for the disobedient, not for the upright.

The catalog of evil men (for whom the law does exist) demonstrates to what depths the society of Paul's day had sunk. The first six offenses are general, arranged in pairs, and directed against God. The eight which follow are specific and directed against man, a similar pattern to the Ten Commandments. The listing of vices is common in Paul's letters (see Gal. 5:19-21 for example) and probably reflects a characteristic of his preaching style.

Although the vices overlap to some extent it will be helpful to touch upon each one briefly. The "law-breakers" are those who deliberately violate accepted rules. The "rebels" are the undisciplined and insubordinate. The "ungodly" have deliberately set themselves against God while the "sinful" are those whose moral standards have collapsed completely. The "unholy" walk roughshod over sacred customs and the "irreligious" desecrate what Barclay calls "the ultimate decencies of life."

15

"Those who kill their fathers or mothers" are pathological criminals and represent one segment—"murderers"—of the next group. The word translated "adulterers" referred in its early usage to male prostitutes. "Perverts" are male homosexuals, especially pederasts. Ancient history provides abundant evidence of the debased morality of the day. Paul did not exaggerate. "Slave traders" (*KJV*, "menstealers") reflects the flourishing first-century trade in stealing and selling slaves. "Liars and perjurers" are those who care nothing for the truth and feel no moral obligation to others.

It is for people like these that the law exists. It serves to restrict and control their wickedness. But righteous people are governed by a radically different principle. For them the restricting influence of law is unnecessary. They live out their lives in a dynamic relationship to "the glorious gospel of the blessed God." Several things are said about this gospel:

It is wholesome. The term "sound doctrine" is used throughout the pastoral epistles but found nowhere else in the New Testament. The gospel is sound in the sense that it gives health (that is what the adjective means literally). Immorality and lawlessness are diseases. The gospel brings and sustains moral and spiritual health.

It "tells of the glory of God in his eternal felicity" (v. 11, *NEB*). In contrast to the law which points up the sinfulness of man, the gospel reveals the glory of God through Jesus Christ His Son. The author of Hebrews says of the Son that He "is the radiance of God's glory and the exact representation of his being" (Heb. 1:3). God is "blessed" not in the sense that we bless Him, but in that He enjoys within Himself the perfection of eternal bliss.

The gospel is entrusted to man. It is a treasure

16

placed in jars of clay (see 2 Cor. 4:7). God has trusted man to spread the good news that He was incarnate in Christ making it possible for us to have fellowship with Him again (see 2 Cor. 5:18,19). Paul's great challenge, and ours, is to take this message to a world in desperate need of its life-giving power.

The purpose of the law is to restrain wickedness. It is intended for evil men, not good men. Good men (those who are declared righteous through faith in Christ) are governed not by law but by a personal relationship to Jesus Christ. This means, for example, that they not only do not kill (that is merely the restriction of the law) but they do not entertain anger towards others (see Matt. 5:21,22). To live in unbroken fellowship with Christ rules out the possibility of personal resentment and hatred. Note that the "gospel" is far more exacting in its ethical demands than is the "law."

To what extent do you feel that today's evangelicals are living according to laws rather than a dynamic relationship to Jesus Christ? When you do something wrong do you feel that you have broken a law or broken a personal trust? How can we increasingly come to realize that we are not governed by law? "Antinomianists" are people who believe they are beyond all moral law. Why is the New Testament *not* antinomian?

Conquered by Grace (1:12-17)

Mention of this "glorious gospel" which God has entrusted to him prompts Paul to take a moment and write about the amazing grace of God—grace that could perform the unbelievable task of changing the church's most fierce opponent into its most dedicated proponent. The chief of sinners has become the champion of the cross!

Paul offers his thanksgiving to "Christ Jesus our

Lord" (v. 12, note the full title). Jesus of Nazareth is not only God's promised Messiah (that is what "Christ" means) but He is Lord of the church as well. He is both Redeemer and Master. Paul gives thanks to his Saviour and Sovereign for at least three reasons:

It is Christ who has given him strength. How would it have been possible for a misguided Jewish rabbi to reverse the entire direction of his life? Read in 2 Corinthians 11:23-29 the hardships that Paul had to endure and the need for divine strength will be clear. The apostle had learned the paradoxical truth that when he was weak then he was strong (see 2 Cor. 12:10). For this he gave thanks.

Christ considered him faithful. It amazed Paul that God would actually place His trust in the very one who had earned the reputation of arch-persecutor of the church. He is deeply grateful for this remarkable display of confidence.

Christ appointed him to His service. After his conversion on the Damascus road Paul was led blind into the city. There a disciple by the name of Ananias restored his sight. God had told Ananias concerning Paul, "This man is my chosen instrument to carry my name before the Gentiles" (Acts 9:15). Paul can never quite get over the wonder of this divine appointment.

From a human standpoint there is no doubt that Paul (or Saul as he was known at that time) was an unlikely candidate for the position he was soon to fill. He freely acknowledges that he was "a blasphemer and a persecutor and a violent man." He had ridiculed and insulted the Christian believers and all they held sacred. He had thrown himself with abandon into the task of stamping out the church. The word translated "violent man" is especially ugly. It de-

18

scribes one who takes sadistic delight in inflicting, without reason, pain and suffering upon others.

Yet, in spite of all this Paul received mercy. Why? Partially because he acted "in ignorance and unbelief." Note that this does not mean that he bore no responsibility for his persecution of the church. Nor does it mean that ignorance is an excuse for sin. What it does mean is that there exists a difference between the willful violation of divine ordinances and actions that stem from lack of knowledge (see Num. 15:22-31). According to Jewish thought there was no sacrifice sufficient to atone for the arrogant sin of an unrepentant person. Paul could receive mercy because he didn't fit into that category.

Whenever the apostle reflected on all that God had done for him he would almost automatically begin to speak of "the grace of our Lord." It was by grace that he was appointed to his office. It was by grace that he became a believer. God had taken the initiative and poured out His abundant grace upon His most belligerent opponent. Paul had been conquered by grace—God's unmerited favor freely bestowed on the undeserving.

Along with God's grace came "faith and love": faith to replace unbelief and love to take the place of cruelty. These gifts are freely given to those in Christ Jesus. (Note: Some understand verse 14 to mean that Paul's experience of the grace of God at the time of his conversion found support and encouragement from the faith and love *of the local believers*.)

In order to call attention to an extremely important point he is about to make, Paul uses the rhetorical formula, "Here is a trustworthy saying that deserves full acceptance" (v. 15). The first half of the formula is also found in 3:1; 4:9; 2 Timothy 2:11; and Titus 3:8, but not elsewhere in the New Testament. It re-

19

minds us of Jesus' "Verily, verily, I say unto you" which occurs so often in John's Gospel.

The important message is that "Christ Jesus came into the world to save sinners" (1 Tim. 1:15). And of course this is exactly what Jesus taught. In Luke 19: 10, for instance, He says, "The Son of Man came to seek and to save what was lost." The purpose of the Incarnation was the redemption of man. The marvel of redemption is that God took the initiative. While other religions picture man as struggling to gain God's favor, the Christian faith teaches that God Himself came to us in Jesus Christ and did for us what we never could have done for ourselves.

The mention of sinners leads Paul to confess that he is "the worst." He is not overstating the case or trying to elicit sympathy by a show of false humility. His confession stems from a rational appraisal of his days of active opposition to the church. He was the number one persecutor of the Christians. Yet—and here's an example of how God can make the best out of a bad situation—he was shown mercy for the express purpose of demonstrating to all who would believe how unlimited is the patience of Christ Jesus. If the chief of sinners can be forgiven then no one is beyond the reach of divine mercy. Paul is an "example" for all who by believing will inherit eternal life.

This unit began with quiet thanksgiving but now will come to a close with an exalted doxology. We can sense the inner rush of gratitude that lays hold of the apostle and must of necessity find expression in an outward declaration of praise and honor to God.

God is, first of all, the eternal King. The Greek text says, "King of the ages." He is sovereign over all the ages from creation to consummation. Everything is under His control. He is immortal—that is, immune from decay—and invisible, unseen. He is the only

20

God, none other exists (older translations read "only wise" but the adjective is not in the original text—it was probably added from the similar expression in Romans 16:27). The doxology ends with the response, "Amen." This would be the congregation's affirmative response to the ascription of honor and glory to God.

Paul freely acknowledges that he was the worst of sinners. Specifically, he was "a blasphemer and a persecutor and a violent man." Yet he received mercy and this serves as evidence of Christ's unlimited patience. In other words, if God accepted Paul, He can accept anyone. From time to time churches bring in special speakers who have been converted out of some socially unacceptable background. Ex-criminals, prostitutes and drug pushers testify to the change that faith in Christ has brought about in their lives.

Do you think there might be some danger to this practice? On what basis could a congregation determine when such a testimony might move from glorifying God for His transforming power to a subtle suggestion that only those who have gone to the depths of sin can experience the completeness of salvation? How often in Paul's other letters does he refer back to his pre-conversion days? Does this suggest any guideline for the use of this particular kind of testimony?

Fighting the Good Fight (1:18-20)

Ever since his very first sentence after the introduction (vv. 3,4) Paul has been involved in a lengthy digression. This is exactly what we've learned to expect from this one whose heart and mind are filled to overflowing with the concerns of the church.

"Son Timothy," he says, "this charge I give you is in line with the prophecies that pointed you out for

21

this role." The early church had its prophets whose function it was to disclose the mind of God in matters relating to the life of the congregation. For instance, at Antioch it was the prophets who, instructed by the Holy Spirit, commissioned Barnabas and Saul for their missionary task (see Acts 13:1-3). In Ephesus a similar group had indicated that Timothy was God's man to provide leadership, especially to correct and counteract the heretical teaching that certain conscience-hardened individuals were foisting upon the church.

Strengthened by these prophecies Timothy is to "fight the good fight" (v. 18). Paul is fond of drawing his metaphors from the military. Fighting is to be taken in the sense of waging a campaign. It is a good and noble calling to wage a campaign against all attempts to pervert the gospel. It requires the same degree of dedication and discipline that we would expect of an army launching a campaign against a military enemy. In the old favorite, "Onward Christian Soldiers," we sing of the church moving forward "like a mighty army." Does it? At times it appears like a beleaguered minority barely holding out. We need to hear again Christ's triumphant declaration that *He will build His church* and "the powers of the underworld shall never overthrow it" (Matt. 16:18, *Williams*).

Timothy is to wage his campaign armed with "faith and a good conscience." He is challenged to maintain confidence in what he believes to be true. He must never surrender the inner assurance that God will emerge victorious. This faith is to be accompanied by a good conscience. Conscience is that inner necessity to judge an action right or wrong. Instructed by Christian truth the conscience is an effective guide for moral decisions. By rejecting conscience some at

22

Ephesus have "shipwrecked their faith." Someone commented that in addition to being a good soldier the Christian must also be a good sailor. Note that it was the decision to override conscience that led to the ruin of faith. Heresy is the child of willful disregard of conscience, not of a troubled intellect.

Hymenaeus and Alexander are two examples of those who have gone wrong. Later we learn that Hymenaeus by claiming the resurrection was already past had helped to destroy the faith of others (see 2 Tim. 2:17,18). Alexander may have been the metalworker mentioned in 2 Timothy 4:14 who did Paul a great deal of harm. Apparently the remedial action taken by the apostle did not fully accomplish its purpose.

What Paul did was to put the men out of the church. The rather cryptic statement is that he "handed [them] over to Satan." To be excluded from the believing congregation meant to be exposed to the malice of Satan. This was thought of in terms of physical distress. The word translated "to be taught" means to learn by punishment. A similar case is mentioned in 1 Corinthians 5:5 where a member of the church is handed over to Satan because of his incestuous relationship with his father's wife.

The purpose of excommunication is to teach men not to blaspheme. Blasphemy is not merely profanity. The term covers all misguided interpretations of Christian truths. To reject the faith in favor of "myths and endless genealogies" (1:3) is to blaspheme what is sacred. While the purpose of excommunication is remedial it appears that some are beyond help.

Timothy is encouraged to fight the good fight. C.S. Lewis speaks of the Christian faith as an invasion. The beachhead was firmly established by the death and resur-

23

rection of Christ. The church is a well-disciplined battalion of shock troops who have as their objective the overthrow of evil in this world and the establishment of righteousness. This calls for dedication, intensive training, carefully planned sorties, and considerable courage.

How does this metaphor of warfare fit what we are doing each week in our local congregations? What about dedication? Do we have intensive training sessions? Do we know what our objective is? Can we recognize the enemy when we see him? Are we all fighting on the same side? Do we conduct ourselves with courage when tempted to deny our commander-in-chief? Describe the ideal Sunday service in terms of a military planning session. Who gives the orders? How do we prepare for battle? What about those who are AWOL (absent without leave)? Would the army be stronger if every soldier were exactly like me?

2

FIRST TIMOTHY TWO

Pray on Behalf of All (2:1-8)

The first thing Paul had in mind in writing to Timothy was to urge him to confront the would-be teachers at Ephesus and demand that they stop their heretical speculations. Now that this is out of the way (chap. 1) he can turn to the main purpose of the letter—instructions on how the church is to conduct itself. The result is not a formal "manual of church order" (as some think). It is a series of instructions on how Christians in a local community should organize themselves in order to worship God and live together in Christian love.

It is significant that prayer is the number one item on Paul's agenda. Before discussing such issues as qualifications for leadership (chap. 3) or what to do about the widows (chap. 5), it is necessary to lay out God's concern for the entire human family. Paul urges that "requests, prayers, intercession and thanksgiving be made for *everyone*" (v. 1, italics added). This breadth of concern is seen in verse 4, "[God] wants all men to be saved," and verse 6,

"[Jesus] gave himself as a ransom for all men," as well. Could it be that the "doctrinally sound" faction of the church had, in opposition to the idle speculations of the false teachers, withdrawn into a clique which made it appear that God was concerned for a select few only? If so, the exhortation to pray for all men shows that such a narrow outlook is wrong.

The four terms Paul uses for prayer are gathered together for rhetorical effect. While they overlap in meaning there is a certain progression in intensity. The third word, "intercession," had become a semi-technical term for gaining entrance to the presence of a king in order to submit a petition. How appropriate for the intercessory prayer of believers who through Christ have access to the throne of grace. By including "thanksgiving" in prayer, Paul reminds us that gratitude for blessings received is the proper setting for new requests (see Phil. 4:6).

While the church is to pray for all men, one group receives special mention, "kings and all those in authority." Remember that at this period in history the Christians were not blessed with a kindly sovereign. The Roman emperor was the notoriously cruel and depraved Nero (A.D. 54-68). Among his many infamous acts was the burning of Rome which he then blamed on the Christians. Yet in spite of such hostility the New Testament urges respect for civil power. "The authorities that exist," writes Paul, "have been established by God" (Rom. 13:1; see also 1. Pet. 2:13, 14). The practical necessity of living within an established system (even though corrupt and at times belligerent) obliges the believer to pray for that system.

The reason that the church is to pray for the authorities is that they (the believers) may live "peaceful and quiet lives in all godliness and holiness." Paul

26

knows that the development of Christian maturity can best take place in an atmosphere of social stability. Believers are to pray that they may live out their days "in a deeply religious and reverent spirit" *(TCNT)*. "Godliness" indicates true reverence for God; "holiness" is the way it works out in life.

This kind of life is good in and of itself. It is also pleasing to God because it supports His redemptive mission in the world. God is not only "our Savior," says Paul; He also "wants all men to be saved."

This statement has been the subject of much discussion in the history of the church. It is especially troublesome for those who stress that God as sovereign accomplishes all that He decrees. How can God be all-powerful if He is unable to accomplish what He wants to do?

One suggestion is that by "all men," Paul means "all men who have been elected." Another is that salvation should be taken in the sense of physical protection (prayer for the authorities is consistent with God's will that society be protected from lawlessness). Some exegetes use this verse to support the doctrine of universal salvation, i.e., since God wants all men to be saved there is no doubt that He will in fact save all.

The statement "all men" is less troublesome when it is not interpreted in light of the later doctrinal disputes of the church (the Calvinist-Arminian debate belongs to the seventeenth century). In Paul's day the Jews believed that God willed the destruction of sinners and the Gnostics were sure that salvation belonged to a favored few. Not so, says Paul. It is God's will that *all* men be saved and come to a full understanding of the truth.

What this truth involves is laid out in the two verses that follow. Many believe that what we have

27

here is part of an ancient creed. The clauses are compact, they have a rhythmic balance and are highly theological.

First is the fundamental tenet of Judaism: There is only one God. "Hear, O Israel: The Lord our God is one God" (Deut. 6:4, *KJV*) was repeated daily by the pious Jew. Since there is but one God there can be but one gospel. The church is to pray for all men because apart from the gospel there is no other way.

Likewise, there is only one mediator between God and man. Both Jew and Gnostic bridged the gap with various sorts of intermediaries. There is, however, only "One who brings God and men together" *(Beck)* and He is Christ Jesus, Himself a man. It is because Jesus shares the humanity of those He represents that He can serve as a mediator. Christian theology has always taught the full humanity of Jesus Christ. He is both God and man.

The creedal statement (if that is what it actually is) proceeds to explain exactly what the mediator has done. In words which echo Jesus' own statement in Mark 10:45 we are told that He gave Himself as a ransom for all men. A ransom is the price paid to buy back some cherished possession. Elsewhere Paul reminded believers that "a great price was paid to ransom [them]" (1 Cor. 6:20, *Knox*). Here he teaches that the ransom was on behalf of all men. So here is another reason why the church should pray for everyone—Christ died for all men. To restrict prayer to anything less than the full scope of Christ's redemptive work would be to dishonor His death and thwart His desire to reach all men.

The final clause of verse 6 is ambiguous but probably means that Christ's death was a testimony given at the appropriate time (see Gal. 4:4) of God's desire that all men be saved.

28

Paul now claims that it was "for this purpose" (v. 7) that he was appointed herald and apostle. Some think that he is referring to his ministry to the Gentiles as proof positive that God wills to save all men. Others (more appropriately I believe) hold that his appointment as herald and apostle is to the proclamation that Christ by His death bridged the gap between God and man making salvation possible for all who believe.

The strong assertion of his truthfulness ("I am telling the truth, I am not lying") which interrupts verse 7 is typical of Paul (see Rom. 9:1; Gal. 1:20). Timothy, of course, would never question Paul's apostleship. But some at Ephesus may have been trying to undermine Timothy by discrediting Paul.

Paul calls himself a "herald" (one who proclaims good tidings), an "apostle" (one sent on a mission), and a "teacher of the true faith" (one who explains and draws out the full implications of the message). The book of Acts and the Pauline epistles testify to the full range of his activities in all three roles. While others ministered primarily to the Jews, Paul's major mission was "to the Gentiles" (see Gal. 2:9).

Paul now (v. 8) returns to the major theme of prayer. He writes that congregational prayer should continue to be the responsibility of the men in the church. This interpretation rests upon (1) the specific reference to sex ("men"), (2) the tense of the Greek infinitive which leads *The Twentieth Century New Testament* to translate, "It should be the custom everywhere for the men to lead the prayers," and (3) the paragraph to follow instructing women to remain silent and submissive in church (they possibly may have begun to take over the men's responsibility to pray).

It is important to note that the principle here transcends the cultural setting in importance. Paul is writing to a culture in which the conduct of worship had been the responsibility of men. The principle, however, is that prayer should be offered on behalf of all, so that all may lead a more tranquil life under "kings and all those in authority" (v. 2). Although the cultural setting has changed, men and women are still to pray according to this principle.

It is critical that prayer be offered by those who are right with God. Men are to "lift up holy hands." The customary way to pray in that day was to stand with arms outstretched and palms upward. Lifting holy hands is explained in context as praying "without anger or disputing." Earlier we learned that the church at Ephesus was infiltrated with false teachers (see 1:3-7). It is not good for the faithful to get involved in arguments. They all too often end up in unnecessary controversy and dissension. This makes it difficult to stand before God lifting up "holy hands."

Paul urges the church to intercede in prayer for those in positions of authority within the realm. They are to pray for kings even though the kings are totally secular and have no special concern for the Christian church. The purpose of such prayer is that believers may live peaceful and quiet lives in godliness and holiness.

In your opinion has the church failed in its obligation to pray for its political and social leaders? How should one pray for a president whose domestic policies are leading the nation toward economic disaster? Have you ever prayed for the secretary of state? Does God want you to? Will He answer your prayer? What do you think would happen if every born-again believer in North America joined in prayer for a specific concern such as the current breakdown of the family in America?

Quietly Receive Instruction (2:9-15)

As the men of the congregation are to carry out their responsibilities with restraint and reverence, so also are the women to conduct themselves with decorum. Specifically they are to dress modestly and not assert themselves when the church gathers to pray.

It is vital that these instructions be understood in the light of social customs of the first century. The place of women at that time was distinctly different from what it is today. Although Jewish society held woman in higher regard than did most cultures, they nevertheless considered her to be at the disposal of man. She had no part in the synagogue and was forbidden to teach. (However this was not the role of Christian women. See 2 Tim. 4:19-21, for example.) In Greek society the woman was more or less confined to her own house. She was not allowed to attend public assemblies. Only women such as the priestesses of the temple of Aphrodite at Corinth were public women—sacred prostitutes who performed their ancient service for the financial benefit of the cult.

Against this background it is not difficult to see why Paul ordered women to "dress modestly, with decency and propriety." The regulation would be especially appropriate for a mixed congregational meeting. Some commentators note that the terms "decency" and "propriety" both have sexual connotations.

Examples of showy and inappropriate adornment are listed as "braided hair ... gold ... pearls ... expensive clothes." Elaborate hairstyles were regularly worn by the fashionable women of the day. It may be that ornaments of gold were worked into the hair. By mentioning specific items Paul is not supplying us with a list of forbidden luxuries while tacitly approving of all others. The point is that women are not to detract from the purpose of the congregational meeting by dressing in such a way as to call attention to themselves.

This does not mean, however, that they should make themselves unattractive. Their beauty is to be of a different sort. They are to adorn themselves with "good deeds." It is Christian character, not outward adornment, that makes a believing woman attractive. Throughout the Pastorals there is a strong emphasis on good works. Apparently doctrine and practice drift apart with alarming ease. Christians need to be reminded that we are "God's workmanship, created in Christ Jesus to do good works" (Eph. 2:20; see also Titus 2:14; Jas. 2:26).

Paul goes on to say that good deeds (acts of kindness and charity) are "appropriate for women who profess to worship God." A different standard exists for those who "lay claim to piety" *(Knox)*. The person who claims to love God is obliged to live on a higher plane. The pagan world has every right to expect more from those who lay claim to supernatural resources and power.

A congregational setting is still in view as Paul adds that women are to "quietly receive instruction with entire submissiveness" *(NASB)*. It appears that some women in the church had used their newly-found freedom in Christ as an opportunity to take over the teaching function in the church. According to rabbinic practice a woman should never teach the Torah, not even to a small child. Women were not rigorously instructed in religion as were men. They received no formal education. In the early Christian church a woman could learn but not teach. She was to remain in submission. By the act of teaching she would be, in a sense, exercising authority over men.

The verb used here may mean "to lord it over."

Paul gives two reasons for restricting the role of women in the church. First, Adam was formed before Eve. The argument is that since God created Adam as the first member of the human family, He intended him to bear the primary responsibility. In the church this means that man is the one who is to teach and exercise authority.

The second reason is that Eve, not Adam, was the one who was deceived. Paul believed that a woman's tendency to be easily deceived disqualified her from assuming leadership. Paul is not implying that Adam was without guilt; Romans 5:12-19 clearly lays the responsibility on Adam for the entrance of sin into the world. He is simply arguing that since women are more easily led astray they should neither teach nor manage the church.

All this falls strange upon modern ears. Women in contemporary culture play an indispensable role in the welfare and development of the church. Apart from the work of women the modern missionary movement would be a century behind. How then should we understand Paul?

We are again reminded that Scripture must always be interpreted against its specific historical and cultural setting. Paul's rules for women must be understood in terms of the broader principles which they express. It is the principle, not some passing expression of the principle, that is central. We must never fall prey to the mistake of transferring a first-century cultural regulation into a twentieth-century setting without first arriving at a clear understanding of the underlying principle. In this case the principle is the desirability of an orderly and well-managed church. Early Christian women were neither educationally nor socially equipped for the management role. To insist that well-informed contemporary Christian women should remain mute in church is to miss the point entirely.

The final verse of the chapter has furrowed many a brow. How could a woman be saved by bearing children? (Note that the *NIV* solves the problem by translating "kept safe" for "saved" so as to imply physical protection. But just exactly how living a virtuous life insures physical safety in childbirth is not clear!) If the verse teaches salvation by procreation, then what about the plight of the unmarried woman?

Of the many approaches, two emerge as more likely: First, taking salvation in a spiritual sense the verse could mean that women will be saved not by assuming leadership responsibilities in the church but by remaining in their divinely appointed place as mothers and continuing in "faith, love and holiness." Paul may be stressing the significance of childbearing in order to disparage the false views of those who "forbid people to marry" (4:3).

Second, salvation may be understood in the general sense of preservation. It is by bearing and rearing children—not by running the church—that woman's contribution to the welfare of society is to be preserved. Her essential role in the early church was carried out in the family, not in the congregation. Her "salvation" lay in motherhood, not in taking over the responsibilities of men, a task for which she was not yet prepared.

In either case, she is to continue "in faith, love and holiness with propriety." She is to be faithful, loving and pure. And in everything she is to exercise balance and good judgment.

Verses 9-11 provide two good examples of the critical need for a thorough knowledge of New Testament backgrounds. Apart from historical context the verses outlaw the wearing of gold, pearls and expensive clothes by women and demand that they utter not a single word when the church gathers to worship. Obviously we pay little or no attention to this instruction. Almost all women wear gold rings and few if any have ever attended church without opening their mouths at some time.

Is the contemporary church, therefore, disobeying God? Should today's congregations revert to their first-century prototype? How do you go about explaining this "violation" of clear biblical teaching? What is the essential principle lying behind the specific injunctions? Explain how this principle should be expressed in the current period of western civilization. How would you answer the retort that since "the word of the Lord stands forever" (1 Pet. 1:25) we have no right to change any of the specific commands of Scripture?

3

FIRST TIMOTHY THREE

What It Takes to Be a Leader (3:1-7)

Paul moves quite naturally from his discussion of how to conduct oneself in church to the question of what qualities are required for church leadership. Don't let chapter divisions in the Bible lead you astray. They do not always introduce an entirely new subject. Our present divisions date back only about 700 years. They are by no means the work of the apostle!

The discussion begins with a sort of standard formula, "Here is a trustworthy saying" (3:1; see also 1:15). What follows is something we can rely upon. It comes in the form of a proverb or generally accepted truth. "If anyone sets his heart on being an overseer, he desires a noble task." It would appear that some in the church didn't think too highly of the job. It wasn't nearly as exciting as the more charismatic gifts which played such an important role in the growth of the early church. To be an apostle, a prophet or a miracle worker placed one at the center of attention. In contrast, to manage the practical affairs of the church was rather mundane. Because of this attitude Paul felt it wise to remind the congregation that to desire the task of general oversight was in fact an honorable ambition.

Older translations use the word "bishop" for this particular church office. More recent translations use titles such as "overseer" *(NIV)*, "superintendent" *(Goodspeed)* or "pastor" *(Williams)*. The problem with "bishop" is that for most readers it suggests a prominent position in a highly developed church structure. This did in fact take place several centuries later, but in Paul's day a "bishop" was simply the person responsible for overseeing the affairs of a local congregation. The Greek word *episkopos*—from which we get the English "episcopal," means a guardian or overseer. It describes the function of the elder or presbyter, other terms for the same office.

What are the basic qualities the office of overseer requires? In the first place he must be "above reproach" (v. 2). His character and conduct are to be free from any obvious moral defects. In the verses that follow (vv. 2-7) we learn by implication what many of these disqualifying defects are.

The overseer must be "the husband of but one wife." This phrase has been understood in different ways. The two most reasonable interpretations are that (1) Paul is counseling against remarriage, or (2) he is requiring faithfulness in the marriage bond. There is considerable evidence that in that cultural period it was considered praiseworthy to remain unmarried after the death of one's spouse. It is better, however, to understand the phrase as stressing the importance of marital fidelity on the part of church leaders. The *New English Bible* translates, "faithful to his one wife."

The words "temperate, self-controlled, respectable" all suggest Christian maturity expressing itself in a well-ordered life. There is no place here for the headstrong or undisciplined. It was especially important that the overseer be hospitable. In those days when there were few suitable accommodations for travelers (most inns were dirty, expensive, and immoral), it was crucial that overseers open their homes to itinerant preachers and teachers. Unless church leaders had extended their hospitality the Christian faith would never have spread as rapidly as it did. Willingness to teach was obviously an essential requirement of the overseer. How could he carry out his total responsibility if he were unable or unwilling to share his knowledge with others?

The overseer must not be "given to much wine" (v. 3). It is not drinking but drunkenness that is condemned. It should be noted, however, that the wine of biblical days was regularly diluted with water and when taken in moderate amounts had no intoxicating effects. It was used in part for medicinal purposes. In 5:23 Paul will urge Timothy to "use a little wine" for his frequent illnesses.

Further, the leader must be gentle, not violent. A "hard drinker" *(Weymouth)* would likely be given to physical violence. If such conduct seems unlikely in a modern church setting we need to remember that early Christian congregations were just emerging from a pagan background. The restraint which has developed over 20 centuries of church history was not available to first-century believers. On some mission fields there is a saying that it takes a second generation Christian to make a real difference.

Phillips translates the last part of verse 3 to read that the overseer must "not be a controversialist" nor "fond of money-grabbing." This agrees with earlier teaching (in chap. 1) about the need of staying clear of meaningless controversy. The love of money disqualifies a man for church leadership. A wise, old counselor once advised young preachers to beware of "women, money and laziness." All three show up in Paul's list of that which disqualifies one for leadership.

Now, in verse 4, comes a requirement that all too often in our day is overlooked or disregarded. A church leader must "manage his own family well." Specifically he must "see that his children obey him with proper respect." It is obvious that if a man is unable to control his own family there is no reason to think that he will be able to carry out the larger responsibility of governing the church (see v. 5). Paul is eminently practical. Prove yourself where you are before taking on a larger task.

Note that it is assumed that the overseer is married and has a family. Family status, while not a requirement for church leadership, would be the normal situation. As translated in the *New International Version* the phrase "with proper respect" indicates how the *children* are to behave toward the father. It may also be translated "with true dignity" (as in *Weymouth*) in which case it would refer to the manner in which the father manages his household. Both observations are appropriate.

The overseer must not be a "recent convert" (v. 6). Here is a piece of advice that the twentieth-century church needs to take more seriously. The tendency to create instant heroes has never been stronger than it is right now. Whenever a famous actor, athlete or politician makes a public confession of his faith in Christ he is besieged by Christian organizations to act as their spokesman, or at least to endorse in some way their program. This is inconsistent with Paul's warning against placing a new believer so quickly into a place of leadership.

The reason is obvious. Such undue attention encourages pride and this leads to judgment. The word translated "conceited" has the literal meaning "to be filled with smoke." The *Amplified New Testament* says of such a person that "he may [develop a beclouded and stupid state of mind] as the result of pride." In this state of befuddled conceit he is likely to "fall under the same judgment as the devil." As Satan lost his princely standing by pride and rebellion, so also is the new believer especially vulnerable to failure and remorse if elevated to leadership so quickly that it will go to his head.

(Note: Some think that "condemnation of the devil," *KJV*, means the judgment that the *devil* will carry out in the experience of the person who is lured into pride.)

A final qualification for leadership is a good reputation with nonbelievers (see v. 7). This may sound strange to those who think of the church as a persecuted minority. Didn't Jesus say that His followers would be hated by the world (see John 15:18,19)? And, in a later letter to Timothy, Paul will write that "everyone who wants to live a godly life in Christ Jesus will be persecuted" (2 Tim. 3:12). The answer is that regardless of how the non-Christian world treats the church in any particular instance, the leadership of the church must continue to conduct itself in such a way as to merit the respect of outsiders. Preachers and others who fail to live out what they profess do irreparable harm to the cause of Christ. The "devil's trap" is the snare laid by Satan for those whose lives encourage scandal. No such borderline individuals are to be overseers. Only those who are "above reproach" (v. 2) need apply.

Most Christians understand their faith as setting them over against the world. Verses such as James 4:4, "Friendship with the world is hatred toward God," are strong reminders that we have been called out of the world to serve the One who was crucified for His sinless life. Against this background the requirement laid down by Paul that overseers must have a good reputation with outsiders sounds strangely out of place.

How do you reconcile these apparently contradictory points of view? In your own Christian experience are you too much an isolationist or are you on too good terms with the world? In what specific area should the Christian be totally distinct from the world and in what ways should he live his life so as to gain the approval of the unbeliever?

Even Assistants Must Qualify (3:8-13)

In the basic sense the term "deacon" describes a person who serves in a menial capacity (see Luke 22:26 and John 12:2 which use related forms of the word: "the one who *serves*"; Martha "*served*"). Stephen and his six colleagues (in Acts 6) were the first "deacons" in the early church, although their responsibilities included evangelism and miracle working as well. Their "serving" consisted of taking charge of the daily distribution of food to the widows of the church. The deacons of Ephesus should be thought of as those who helped the overseers, especially in the more general and mundane tasks.

It is widely known that the Jews of that day had carefully worked out systems to provide for the needy. Just before the Sabbath, men from the synagogue would make the rounds to collect donations of food and see that it got to the poor. This concern for the needy was carried over into the Christian church. To the deacons fell the responsibility of putting it into practice.

41

In spite of the fact that deacons were called upon to serve the congregation in what might appear to be unimportant tasks, the requirements for the office were quite similar to those of the overseers. They were to be "men worthy of respect" (v. 8; see v. 4) and "sincere." Literally translated the phrase is "not double-tongued." It could refer to the tendency to gossip and carry tales from house to house (a real temptation for those whose responsibilities kept them in constant contact with the entire church) or, more probably, to the temptation to say one thing to one person but something else to the next. John Bunyan (in *Pilgrim's Progress*) talks about "Mr. Two-tongues," a parson in the town of Fair-speech. Nothing will tear a church apart quicker than busybodies who spend their time and energy carrying tidbits of information between members of the congregation.

Like the overseer, the deacon must not be given to excessive drinking or "money-grubbing" *(NEB)*. In both areas the warnings are given in stronger terms to the deacons. This does not imply a double standard. Every overseer was probably first a deacon and therefore it would be necessary only to restate the requirement. Since a deacon distributed money as well as food to the poor, it was essential that he not be a greedy person. The temptation to pilfer would be too great.

Deacons are to "keep hold of the deep truths of the faith with a clear conscience" (v. 9). It is important that the fundamentals of the Christian faith be maintained without compromise. It is equally important that correct doctrine be accompanied by a clear conscience. All too often the church has inadvertently furnished examples of how to be theologically orthodox yet ethically questionable.

The word translated "deep truths" is an important

term in Pauline thought. A more literal translation is "mystery" (Greek, *mustērion*). A biblical "mystery" is not something obscure or unknown. It refers to a truth, formerly hidden, but now revealed to those who will accept it by faith. For example, in Colossians 1:27 Paul speaks of "this mystery, which is Christ in you, the hope of glory" (see also Rom. 16:25). In 1 Timothy 3:9 *(KJV)* it is the "mystery of the faith," the basic truths that constitute the Christian faith (e.g., the incarnation, vicarious death, and bodily resurrection of Jesus Christ). Deacons must hold to these fundamental truths and maintain a pure conscience. Theology and morality can never be separated without fatal damage to either or both.

Before a deacon is allowed to serve he is to be tested (see v. 10). This provision could refer to a probationary period during which time the church leaders would pay careful attention to the life and service of the candidate. It is more probable, however, that the "testing" refers to an appraisal of the candidate in terms of the qualifications which are being set out.

Only if there is "nothing against them" are the candidates to serve as deacons. Every qualification is of vital importance. If the candidate meets every requirement (in v. 8-10) except one—let's say, for example, a weakness towards wine—that one exception is enough to disqualify him. It is often noted that *deacons*, but not overseers, were to be tested. This does not mean that the more responsible position had lower requirements. As noted earlier, we may reasonably assume that men became deacons (servants of the congregation in practical tasks) before they were promoted to the more important role of overseer. The crucial test would be at the point of entry into congregational office. Whether or not a deacon should be advanced to a more prominent role would be clearly demonstrated by the manner in which he carried out his responsibilities in the lesser role.

Verse 11 is a parenthesis in the middle of the discussion on deacons (vv. 8-13). Commentators are about evenly divided on whether the women spoken of are (1) wives of the deacons, or (2) women deacons. *Phillips* translates, "Their wives should share their serious outlook." *Williams* has, "The deaconesses too must be serious." All the Greek text says, literally, is, "women/wives similarly grave, not slanderers . . . " Some suggest that the admonition is directed toward the women of the congregation in general, but this raises the question of why such a parenthesis would be inserted in the middle of Paul's list of qualifications for deacons.

My suggestion is that the women in question are both the wives of the deacons and in some sense therefore "deaconesses." While the formal office of deaconess did not develop until a later period (especially the third and fourth centuries), women served from the beginning in visiting the sick and needy and in helping in the preparation of women candidates for baptism. In Romans 16:1 Phoebe is called a servant or deaconess (Greek, *diakonos*). Elsewhere Paul commends Euodia and Syntyche for helping in the cause of the gospel (see Phil. 4:3). It would be most appropriate for the deacons at Ephesus to be accompanied by their wives in many of their services to the congregation.

The qualities required of these women are much the same as those for deacons. They are to be serious-minded, temperate and absolutely dependable. The only new item is "not malicious talkers." The same word (Greek, *diabolos*) is translated appropriately in both verse 6 and 7 as "devil." It means "slanderer."

44

Satan is *the slanderer* par excellence. Women in the service of the church are not to be "she-devils," malicious scandalmongers.

Like the overseer, the deacon must be a faithful. husband (see 3:2) and have proven his ability to manage well both his "children and his household" (v. 12; see 3:4,5). The deacon who has served well will be rewarded in two ways (see v. 13):

First, *he will "gain an excellent standing."* This does not mean promotion to a higher office (hardly an appropriate motive for loving service as a deacon) but to the esteem and influence within the congregation that naturally results from a job well done. One writer puts it well, "Influence is a by-product of character" (Simpson). This runs counter to man's natural tendency to pursue influence even though it may demonstrate an essential lack of character.

The second reward is *"great assurance in their faith in Christ Jesus."* Those who serve well will enjoy great boldness towards both man and God. When men faithfully carry out the tasks that God assigns they find themselves possessed of a greater confidence in the reality and truth of the Christian faith. Inactive believers are wide open to doubt. To serve well is to enjoy the freedom of faith.

Paul writes that deacons are to hold the deep truths of the faith with a clear conscience. We need to examine what this means.

What it means to maintain the truth of the gospel is perfectly clear. We are to continue in our confidence that the basic truths of the life, death and resurrection of Christ are absolutely reliable. But these theological truths have ethical implications. That is, the death of Christ on my behalf lays upon me an obligation to live a different kind of life. This is where conscience enters.

Am I, in fact, living out in daily conduct the moral obligations that flow from the "deep truths of the faith"? To what extent does my conscience witness to a life of active holiness which stems from my relationship to a Creator and Redeemer who is holy (see 1 Pet. 1:15,16)? Since the conscience can be hardened by willful sin, to what extent is it a dependable guide to conduct? Will the Christian ever sin as a result of following his conscience? How do you think the conscience of the believer has been altered by virtue of his new birth?

What It's All About (3:14-16)

This short paragraph in verses 14 to 16 stands at the heart of Paul's letter. Not only does it separate the discussions on prayer and qualities for leadership from the three chapters of practical directions that follow, but it also states (1) the purpose of the letter (how the family of God is to behave itself), and (2) the theological basis for the letter's instructions.

The apostle indicates that he hopes to come to Ephesus soon (see v. 14), but is writing ahead so that in case of delay they may have in hand his instructions on how the congregation is to live together in love. By this time in Paul's life he has learned that his times are in God's hands. He would agree with James that a man ought to say, "If it is the Lord's will, we will live and do this or that" (Jas. 4:15).

It should be noted that in the original text there is no way of determining whether 1 Timothy 3:15 is speaking of how *Timothy* is to conduct himself or how the *church* is to behave itself. But the *New International Version* (and most translations) is probably correct in taking the second alternative. Having traveled with Paul since the start of the second missionary journey, Timothy would certainly have known how *he* should conduct himself. Besides, the instructions in the letter deal primarily with conduct appropriate for the church at large.

The church, quite obviously, is not the church building. It is that body of believers who have been "called out" (that's what the word means) of the world to enjoy a spiritual fellowship with God and one another, made possible by the death and resurrection of Jesus Christ. The church is designated as "God's household," that is, the family of God. One of the most exciting things about belonging to God is the realization that we are one great family spread throughout the nations of the entire world. As a missionary in Central America I remember the thrill of being accepted into the fellowship of a group of believers whose skin color was different from mine and whose language I was just beginning to understand. God's household has no ethnic or racial divisions. We are brothers in Christ and children alike of the living God.

Finally, Paul says the church is "the pillar and foundation of the truth" (v. 15). The problem with this statement as translated is that it seems to say that the truth rests upon, or has its basis in, the church. Actually, the opposite is true. Jesus Christ is the only foundation (see 1 Cor. 3:11) and it is upon this foundation that the church is built (Matt. 16:18). The problem is less when we note (1) that the original text does not say "*the* pillar" but rather "a pillar," and (2) that "foundation" is better translated "bulwark" or "buttress" indicating that which supports or holds up. The truth does not depend upon the church for its validity. Truth is by definition that which corresponds to reality. Reality in this case is what God did in Christ to reconcile the world to Himself (see 2 Cor. 5:19). The church, however, is a "pillar" and "buttress" to the truth in the sense that it supports and defends it against the assaults of false teachers (see 1 Tim. 1:3,4,19,20).

Mention of the truth draws from Paul the almost ecstatic exclamation, "Great beyond all question is the mystery of our religion" (1 Tim. 3:16, *NEB*). Some find here an echo of the mob in Ephesus who, upon being stirred up by Demetrius the silversmith, cried out, "Great is Artemis of the Ephesians" (Acts 19:28,34). The "mystery of godliness" (1 Tim. 3:16, *NIV*) is the truth now revealed that calls forth from man a life of godly conduct.

The essence of the Christian faith is set forth by means of a primitive hymn. It consists of six lines that may be divided into three couplets of two lines each. Furthermore, each couplet consists of an antithesis or comparison.

Those who are accustomed to reading the *King James Version* will note that the opening word "God" is regularly replaced in modern translations with a pronoun that relates the entire poem to Christ. Manuscript evidence for "God" is weak and late. The content of the hymn quite obviously deals with Christ the Son.

The hymn teaches, in the first place, the reality of the Incarnation. The eternal Son of God entered into His own created universe and was "made visible in human form" *(Williams)*. Jesus Christ was genuinely man. He was part and parcel of the human race. Who can plumb the depths of the mystery of the Incarnation?

Yet He was "vindicated by the Spirit." Although He took the form of a servant He was declared to be "the Son of God by his resurrection from the dead" (Rom. 1:4), a mighty act wrought in the power of the Spirit (see Rom. 8:11).

The next couplet in 1 Timothy 3:16 teaches that

48

Christ was "seen by angels" and "preached among the nations." On the one hand His vindication is celebrated in heaven by angels around the throne who sing, "Worthy is the Lamb, who was slain" (Rev. 5:11,12). Meanwhile on earth the Resurrection is proclaimed to men of every nation (see Acts 2:5,24, 31,32).

The final two lines in 1 Timothy 3:16 reverse the order of the second couplet. As a result of being "preached among the nations" Christ is "believed on in the world." In order to be "seen by angels" he must be "taken up in glory." The innumerable angels around the throne in Revelation 5 declare the Lamb to be worthy "to receive power and wealth and wisdom and strength and honor and glory and praise!" (Rev. 5:12). This is what it means to be "taken up in glory."

There exists no finer example of an early Christian hymn of adoration than 1 Timothy 3:16. It reveals the early Christian church's exalted understanding of Christ. It should serve as a model for all hymnody. We need to sing once again the praises of Christ our Lord. Our modern fixation on how *we* feel about everything spiritual betrays an unfortunate concern about self.

The "household" of God (v. 15) is the family of God. Families, in order to exist as social units, have to follow certain rules. For example, if the members of a household never ate together or shared their lives with one another they could hardly be called a family. Rules are not created in order to deprive children of a good time but to insure that the family as a whole conducts itself in such a way that the result is to the greatest mutual advantage.

The church is the family of God. What kind of rules are most appropriate for the maximum spiritual benefit of the entire family? List a few. Who ultimately decides proper conduct in God's family? Where do we find these instructions? What is man's role in working out an acceptable pattern of conduct for the church? Who, if anyone, should administer correction in the church family? What are the greatest benefits that derive from our membership in God's family? How should the concept of family affect our relationship to one another?

4

FIRST TIMOTHY FOUR

Latter-Day Legalism (4:1-5)

Jewish thought divided history into two ages: "this age" and "the age to come." The present age was thought of as under the control of Satan. The age to come was the messianic era of peace and universal righteousness.

The Christian church viewed itself as existing in a transition period between the two ages. The great victory over the powers of evil had already taken place with the resurrection of Jesus Christ. Yet the universal acknowledgement of this victory awaited His triumphant return. Immediately preceding this return would be a time of great travail and tribulation. It would be a period of false prophets and heretical teachings.

For Paul these last days were to be times of apostasy. In fact, the heresies at Ephesus were an obvious indication that the end of history was at hand. This is the clear teaching of the Spirit (see 1 Tim. 4:1). There will be those who rebel against the faith and follow after deceiving spirits. They will be taken in by doctrines that are demonic in origin.

51

None of this should come as a surprise. Did not Jesus speak of the last days when "many false prophets will appear and deceive many people" (Matt. 24:11)? And when Paul met with the Ephesian elders at Miletus did he not warn of "savage wolves" from without who would not "spare the flock" and men from within who would "distort the truth" (Acts 20:29,30)? These predictions have come true and Timothy must deal with the problem.

The next point (1 Tim. 4:2) that Paul makes is of critical importance. While the heresies of the last days are demonic in origin they will be spread abroad by human teachers. These men are "hypocritical liars." Although what they say is untrue, the way they say it leaves the impression of high and lofty motives. Heresy is normally a twisted truth rather than an outright lie. It is this lingering presence of truth (even though altered) that deceives the unwary. The false teachers are liars because what they teach is untrue, and hypocrites because they pretend it isn't.

How can people do this? Because, according to *Phillips'* translation, their "consciences are as dead as seared flesh." This understands the phrase in the sense of Ephesians 4:19 where pagans are pictured as "having lost all sensitivity." Their consciences have been "cauterized" (the Greek is *kauteriazō*). Others take the expression in 1 Timothy 4:2 to mean that the conscience has been "branded" (*NEB* says, "branded with the devil's sign"). In antiquity, slaves were sometimes branded on the forehead to indicate ownership. In either case evil men have sold out to Satan and have become willing tools for his malicious twisting of the truth. That these heretics were received within the church fellowship and allowed to spread their pernicious doctrine reveals the constant danger that faces the Christian fellowship in every age.

52

The heretics were pressing two particular points. First, that people should not marry (see v. 3). Paul had counseled in an earlier letter and on an entirely different basis that in view of "the present crisis" it would be better to refrain from marriage (see 1 Cor. 7:26; see also vv. 29-31). But here the prohibition is based upon the Gnostic point of view that since the human body is material and therefore evil, its natural relationships should be severely curtailed. Paul doesn't bother to refute such an obvious error.

In the second place, the false teachers would deny to believers certain foods (see 1 Tim. 4:4). The real issue at stake is the character of God. Is God essentially a being who requires man to deny the world in which he lives or would He have us accept with thanksgiving all that creation offers? Does being a Christian consist in not doing certain prescribed things or in gratefully partaking of all that is in fact good and appropriate? Paul opts for the second alternative. But note especially the place of thanksgiving: Those who believe and know the truth receive with thanksgiving all the many and varied gifts of God. That is why He created them in the first place.

Everything created by God is good because God Himself is good. This is the fundamental principle. After the six days of creation, "God saw all that he had made, and it was very good" (Gen. 1:31). Nothing, therefore, is to be rejected if it is received with thanksgiving.

Lest the modern reader misapply this basic truth it is well to remind ourselves that the context of Paul's remarks has to do with food that was considered *ceremonially* unclean. It was a question of taboos. By stating that no man is made "unclean" by what enters him Jesus declared all foods "clean" (Mark 7:18,19). Peter's vision at Joppa dramatized the same point (see Acts 10:9-16). Obviously there are other restrictions on foods that have nothing to do with ceremonial considerations. Spoiled fish and rotten eggs are not good for dinner even if you say the blessing over them!

The thanksgiving Paul refers to is what is commonly called "grace" before meals. Giving thanks was a regular custom observed by Jesus (see Mark 6:41; Luke 24:30). The ceremonial taboos of the non-Christian should have no place in the lives of the believers. The word of thanks believers offer to God for His gifts of food consecrates the meal. It is in this way set aside so as to serve a holy purpose.

The act of thanksgiving is described as consisting of "the word of God and prayer" (1 Tim. 4:5). The two elements should be taken together to mean the blessing pronounced upon that which is about to be eaten. It is the appropriate response to God for His goodness in what may at times appear to be relatively insignificant. We are reminded that the practice of grace before meals is honoring to God and a safeguard against ingratitude on the part of man.

Certain people at Ephesus taught that marriage was wrong and that serious Christians shouldn't eat foods that they had blacklisted. It all sounds terribly spiritual, doesn't it! The road to "super sainthood" leads through the grim land of self-denial. Paul knew that the approach of asceticism produces pride rather than godliness. He knew that what God created is good and should be received with thanksgiving.

The obvious question is: What are the appropriate limits to this apparently blanket statement that appears to declare everything to be good? God, through the natural processes of growth and fermentation, produces wine. Should we praise God and drink up? Since sexual desire is an inherent part of our physical makeup are we to allow it total freedom? If not, why not? If it is true that any single portion of Scripture is to be interpreted in light of all other Scripture what natural qualifications should attend our interpretation of verse 4?

Developing Spiritual Muscles (4:6-10)

The rest of chapter 4 is loaded with practical advice. Although directed toward the specific needs of the young minister Timothy and the situation at Ephesus, it has much to say to his twentieth-century counterparts who labor in the ministry of the gospel. Note that the counsel is positive. Paul knows how useless it is to engage in philosophical argument about the validity of this or that tenet of religious error. The answer to heresy is a positive setting-forth of the Christian faith coupled with an exemplary life.

Being "a good minister" (4:6) (or servant; same word as "deacon" in 3:8) of Christ involves pointing "these things out to the brothers." The verb is a gentle one and carries the idea of suggesting rather than ordering. The best kind of leadership is not dictatorial but, as the word suggests, *lead*-ership. Men are motivated most strongly by what emerges from within, not what is demanded from without. A real leader helps others arrive at what they instinctively know is best. Note the family affection in the word "brothers." The church is not rigidly structured like an unwieldy corporation with levels of management. It is primarily a family of believers who have committed themselves to God and to one another.

Two additional characteristics of a good minister are mentioned:

First, *he continues to nourish himself with the great central truths of the faith.* As Jeremiah said, "When your words came, I ate them; they were my joy and

55

my heart's delight" (Jer. 15:16). The Word of God is absolutely crucial to effective Christian service. George Müller of the famed Bristol Orphanage wrote, "The vigor of our Spiritual Life will be in exact proportion to the place held by the Bible in our life and thoughts. I solemnly state this from the experience of fifty-four years."

Second, the life of the minister *must measure up to the ethical standards he proclaims.* Timothy had "faithfully followed" (1 Tim. 4:6, *Weymouth*) the good teaching of the faith. In the long run no man can preach better than he lives. And good preaching is borne out of faithful commitment to the Word and all that it implies about life and conduct.

If a minister is nourishing his soul on the good truths of the faith he will have no need to busy himself with the "godless myths" (v. 7) of every new heresy. Paul calls them "old wives tales" by way of derision. They are believable only to superstitious old women.

In marked contrast Timothy is to train himself in godliness (see v. 8). That godly living involves the manly art of self-discipline comes as a surprise to those who think of religion as producing passive and inoffensive nonentities. To the contrary, godly living demands the same kind of rigorous striving for goals as found among athletes of the highest calibre. We admire the professional athlete and marvel at his ability to subject all other interests to the disciplined pursuit of achieving his goal. We should transfer this same dedication, says Paul, to the goal of spiritual fitness.

Physical training is of some benefit but godliness is of value in every way. Specifically it carries with it the promise of life both now and hereafter. The King James's "bodily exercise profiteth little" is unfortunate in that it seems to suggest that there is little or no value in physical training. This is not what Paul says. His comparison is between the limited value of physical fitness and the unlimited value of spiritual fitness. Godliness is valuable because it makes the present life a more abundant life (see John 10:10) and it guarantees continuous fellowship with Christ in the age to come.

Once again in 1 Timothy 4:9 we meet the standard formula that introduces a widely accepted saying (see also 1:15 and 3:1). The formula reminds us that what is about to be said is absolutely trustworthy and "entitled to the fullest acceptance" *(Goodspeed)*. In a day when all sorts of ideas and alien philosophies are competing for the mind of man it is good to have a sure word from beyond. The statement in verse 10, "And for this we labor and strive," points back to verse 8 with its reference to the life to come. It continues the athletic metaphor and indicates that godly living requires exertion and total dedication.

You may ask how this can be harmonized with the idea of "resting in the Lord" which is found elsewhere in the New Testament. The "rest" of faith has to do with our conviction that no amount of activity can displace the role of simple trust. But trust does not mean inactivity. Trust is a continuing act of the will. While it is not a substitute for action it does move us to appropriate action. A godly life is built upon complete trust in God expressed in the strenuous activity which that relationship calls forth.

We labor and strive, says Paul, precisely *because* "we have put our hope in the living God." Our continuous attitude of hope (not an isolated act) provides the basis for our "toiling and wrestling" *(Weymouth)*. Why train in godliness if there is no validity to our religious beliefs? On the other hand, if the Christian faith is true then how could anyone do less than give his very best?

Paul refers to God as "the Savior of all men, and especially of those who believe." If this refers to salvation in the normal sense of being accepted as righteous, then it would teach that all men will ultimately be saved. This, of course, would be contrary to the clear teaching of the New Testament. What the statement means is that God is the only one who can save men and this salvation is in fact accomplished in the lives of those who believe. *Moffatt* translates, " 'God, the Saviour of all men'—of believers in particular." It is possible that the word is being used in a double sense—God is in a general sense the *Preserver* of all men, and in a spiritual sense the *Saviour* of those who believe.

Let's think together about what is involved in training in godliness. We are dealing with an athletic metaphor. Paul knew all about the games and contests that were part of Greek life. He undoubtedly admired the strenuous exertion and singleness of mind that went into the making of a champion. What about training in godliness, he pondered. Should not the demand for spiritual fitness call forth from the church the same degree of personal commitment?

How would you describe a spiritually flabby Christian? What sort of person would he be? Physical training follows a regular schedule. List some spiritual exercises that would get the church into better shape. Is godliness important? Is it as important for the Christian to be in shape spiritually as it is for the athlete to stay in shape physically? Who among your acquaintances has the best spiritual fitness? What does he do to stay in shape that you don't do? Are you willing to pay the price in self-discipline for spiritual fitness?

Stick to Your Calling (4:11-16)

It would appear that Timothy was a somewhat timid young man, hesitant to assert himself as he might in the affairs of the congregation. This impression is strengthened by Paul's remark to the believers at Corinth that, "if Timothy comes, see to it that he has nothing to fear" (1 Cor. 16:10). Reference to his youth in 1 Timothy 4:12 has no necessary bearing on the subject because the Greek word could be used of anyone of military age, that is up to about 40. Timothy was probably born about the time Christ died. This would place him in the mid-30s at the time of the letter. On the other hand, he was younger in a *relative* sense than the Ephesian elders and this may have led some of them to question the validity of his leadership and authority.

In any case, Paul instructs his young colleague to "command and teach these things." In correcting error he is to speak with authority. The charge has a military ring. "Pass on these orders" is the *New English Bible* translation. Timothy is not to let anyone "look down on" him (think disparagingly or treat with contempt) because he was younger or perhaps because he had not been a member of the congregation as long as others. Instead, he is to set an example. As Barclay says, he is to "silence criticism by conduct." The immediate reaction of most of us toward unfair criticism is to mount a heated defense of our integrity and accomplishments. The quality of a person's life, however, is his most eloquent defense. Live in such a way as to prove to all the falseness of the charges laid against you. In so doing you will not only demonstrate your own integrity but you will "set an example for the believers."

The example needs to be set in five areas:

Be an example in speech. James knew the difficulty

59

of this requirement. He recommended that "everyone should be slow to speak" (1:19) because the tongue "is a restless evil, full of deadly poison" (3:8). It was especially important that Timothy's speech be "full of grace, seasoned with salt" (Col. 4:6).

In life. The word means "way of life, conduct, behavior." It is what we today call "life-style." Timothy is to live in such a way as to allow him to say, as Paul said, "Follow my example, as I follow the example of Christ" (1 Cor. 11:1).

In love. Christian love is overcoming selfishness in order to care for others. It is basically an act of the will. When a believer *decides* to serve others, the Holy Spirit provides the power.

In faithfulness. The word "faith" can mean trust in an active sense or the reliability on which trust is built. In this context the second alternative is to be preferred.

In purity. This requirement for spiritual leadership is especially appropriate in the mid-twentieth century when the marvels of electronic communication can bring all sorts of morally questionable "entertainment" into our homes. To submit ourselves willingly to whatever the networks have decided is necessary to sell products is to retreat from the standard of purity that Christ requires. Paul counseled believers at Philippi to think on those things which were true, noble and pure (see Phil. 4:8).

Paul intends to return to Ephesus but in the meantime Timothy is to carry out the three basic functions of public worship:

First, he is to *devote himself to the "public reading of Scripture"* (1 Tim. 4:13). The Christian worship service is oriented primarily to the Word of God written. This is why many churches insist on placing the pulpit in the center of the worship area. The practice of reading the Old Testament aloud was taken over from the synagogue (see Luke 4:16). In Christian congregations the writings of the apostles were added to the Jewish Scriptures (see Col. 4:16). The office of public reader (or *lector*) developed because of the technical difficulty of reading Hebrew script which omitted vowels and made no separation between words.

Timothy is also to *devote himself* "to preaching and to teaching" (1 Tim. 4:13). Preaching is the exhortation that follows and is based upon the Scripture read. It encourages listeners to be "doers of the word, and not hearers only" (Jas. 1:22, *KJV*). Truth that results in action opens the way for further understanding. Truth that does not issue in action numbs the soul and retards spiritual growth. It is "dangerous" to hear God speak.

Teaching, the third element in public ministry, refers to *catechetical instruction on the great central truths of the Christian faith.* The creedal fragments in 1 Timothy 1:17 and 3:16 could be a part of this teaching. In a day when heresy was threatening Christian orthodoxy it was supremely important for believers to know with certainty the fundamental truths of their faith. Correct theology is still the best antidote for error even today.

Timid people do not seek authority over others. Explaining Scripture and exhorting the brethren (see 4:13) was apparently not what Timothy would have chosen. Yet God had given him the special spiritual endowment for this task. This *charisma*, or spiritual gift, came to him at the time of his ordination when the elders laid hands upon him. In Jewish custom this rite goes back to the commissioning of Joshua. Moses was ordered by God to have Joshua stand before Eleazar the priest and there before all the congregation he was to lay his hands upon him. In so doing Moses would "give him some of [his] authority" (Num. 27:20). The custom was followed in the synagogue for the ordination of rabbis and carried over into the Christian church (see Acts 6:6; 13:3).

Timothy received the *charisma* "under the guidance of prophecy" (1 Tim. 4:14, *NEB*). God's Spirit made it clear to the elders that Timothy had received the necessary spiritual endowment to carry out the leadership role in the congregation. Paul reminds his young helper of this fact and charges him not to neglect his gift. It was given for the benefit of others (see 1 Cor. 12:7) and was intended to be used.

Further exhortations follow. Timothy is to "be diligent in these matters" (1 Tim. 4:15)—that is, he is to "give [himself] wholly to them." The immediate reference would be to the duties just described in the previous paragraph. An alternate translation of the first clause of verse 15 is "meditate upon these things" *(KJV)*. In this case the exhortation would relate primarily to verse 13 the teaching and preaching of Scripture. Although this is instructive it is more likely that Paul is continuing the athletic metaphor of verse 7.

"Give yourself wholly to them" (v. 15) literally translated is, "Be in these things." Timothy is to become totally absorbed into his ministry. It is to be his life, his very existence. The purpose is "so that everyone may see your progress." Christian maturity is pictured as a journey. It begins at conversion and continues to the end of this life. The life of a Christian leader should be open and transparent for all to see. It should involve progress along a well-established road from sinful self-centeredness to loving service for others.

All too often a congregation expects "perfection"

of its minister. Any flaw is either overlooked as not being there or becomes the occasion for great disappointment. Such a person can never be an "example" because we cannot relate to him except in his failure. Better to acknowledge the frailty of all and look for progress rather than "perfection."

Timothy is to "keep a critical eye" (v. 16, *Phillips*) on his life and on his doctrine. Balance is needed. Undue concentration on "life" leads to emotional instability. If one is always taking his spiritual temperature it will rise automatically. Attention to doctrine alone, however, leads to intellectual arrogance.

Stick to it, says Paul, and you will "save both yourself and your hearers." Salvation is a comprehensive term indicating deliverance. Unfortunately we sometimes limit it to what happens at the moment of conversion. But not only *were* we saved, we are still *in the process* of being saved. (See Charles K. Barrett's discussion on 1 Cor. 15:2 in his *First Epistle to the Corinthians*, New Testament Commentaries, vol. 9, Harper & Row Publishers.) Sanctification is the process by which the believer is "conformed to the likeness of [God's] Son" (Rom. 8:29). This supernatural transformation is made possible by the Spirit of God who lives within the believer. But our active willingness is required to allow the change to take place. It is in this sense that we "save ourselves." Timothy is to persevere in all the instructions he has just received from Paul. If he follows through faithfully he will save himself and help others to be delivered from this "present evil age" (Gal. 1:4).

As the "pastor" of the church at Ephesus, Timothy is instructed by Paul to devote himself to "the public reading of Scripture, to preaching and to teaching." This was his gift and therefore his primary responsibility.

Is this same emphasis upon explaining Scripture and exhorting the brethren appropriate for today's ministers? Should it still be central? Aren't modern churches so large and complex that the minister ought to shift his priorities to administration and pulpiteering? Is God's Word actually central in your congregation? How much of the morning service is given over to keeping the organization running smoothly? What could be dropped and what might be added?

5

FIRST TIMOTHY FIVE

The Family of Believers (5:1,2)

Just when and how it is appropriate to correct another person has always been a problem. Normally we shy away from it. And many a person has ended up in sorrow or disgrace because no one was willing to say a word of caution. Yet Christian love requires the willingness to correct. It is a special concern of leadership and calls for both wisdom and tact.

Older men are not to be severely reprimanded (see 5:1). In earlier times age was honored. It would be inappropriate for a young minister like Timothy to scold or rebuke harshly an elderly man in the church. Rather he is to appeal to him as he would to his own father. The same attitude of loving consideration is to be extended to younger men as well. Treat them with brotherly affection. Harshness is out of place. Paul would agree that "kindness toward others is the rent we pay for our room here on earth."

Older women are to be treated as mothers and younger women as sisters (see v. 2). With the latter

group Timothy is to show all modesty. Taylor paraphrases rather bluntly, "thinking only pure thoughts
about them." Paul is perfectly aware of those problems which can arise in what appears to be the most
innocent situations. Wise pastors know that the in-
timacy of a counseling session often provides temptations of the most dangerous sort.

Correction requires both insight and tact. One indication
of Christian maturity is a sensitive regard for the feelings
and welfare of others in the church.

How would you correct an older man whose conduct
was affecting the young people adversely? Let's say he
is rather open and unashamed about his questionable
business practices. He takes unfair advantage of others
and brags about it. Does anyone have the responsibility
of bringing this to his attention? In what spirit should it be
done? Since pastors (such as Timothy) are to treat
"younger women as sisters, with absolute purity," what
practices normally followed by society in general should
be avoided by the minister? What merit is there (if any) in
a pastor taking his wife along when counseling unmarried
women? Is this prudish or wise?

How to Tell a "Real Widow" (5:3-8)
Readers are sometimes surprised by the amount of
attention Paul gives to widows at this point. For the
next 14 verses he will be laying out instructions for
their conduct and welfare.

It is well at the outset to distinguish in these verses
(3-16) three kinds of widows: (1) there are widows
who belong to a family unit: they have children or
grandchildren who can care for them (see v. 4); (2)
there are "younger widows" who should remarry (vv.
11-15,6); (3) there are official widows of the church
(see vv. 3-5,9,10). These "congregational widows"

may have constituted a regular order in the church and have carried out a specific function. More about them as we go along.

In the Old Testament special concern was expressed for the widow. David sings the praises of God as "Father to the fatherless, a defender of widows" (Ps. 68:5). Isaiah exhorts the people of God to "defend the cause of the fatherless, plead the case of the widow" (Isa. 1:17). The same concern is seen in the New Testament where deacons were appointed in the Jerusalem church to take care of the daily distribution of food to widows (see Acts 6:1). True religion has always had a sensitive social conscience (see Jas. 1:27).

Paul instructs Timothy to "give proper recognition" to the widow "who is alone in the world" (1 Tim. 5:5, *NEB*). Older translations use "honor" which emphasizes appropriate respect. But in addition to respect they are to receive material support. This requires official recognition as having met the requirements listed in verses 5, 9 and 10. From the larger context we gather that "real widows" were those in genuine need (alone in the world) and who had accepted a ministry of prayer (see v. 5) and kindly service to others (see v. 10).

If, however, a widow had "children or grandchildren" (v. 4, not "nephews" as the *KJV* has it) then it would be the responsibility of the family, not the church, to care for them. Throughout the Greek world it was widely accepted that children should provide for their parents. Demosthenes, the great Athenian orator, held that anyone neglecting his parents was hateful to both the gods and to men. Aristotle taught that a person should starve rather than let his parents go without food. If this is what the pagan world accepted as one's moral (and legal) responsibil-

67

ity how could the church allow anything less? Children are to put their religion into practice. They are to care for their own family (and this would certainly include a widowed mother!) and in this way repay their obligation to those who brought them up. This kind of tangible concern, says Paul, "is pleasing to God." It fulfills the fifth commandment ("Honor your father and mother") which carries with it the promise of success and the enjoyment of long life (see Eph. 6:1-3). Paul the theologian is also Paul the man of practical concern.

In contrast to widows who have children to care for them are the "real widows" (v. 5), that is, women who are alone in the world and without any means of support. For these the church has an obligation. They are characterized as (1) having fixed their hope upon God and (2) as continuing in prayer night and day. Without family to fall back on the "real widow" has cast herself upon the goodness of God who is the protector of widows. While such a widow undoubtedly was always in the attitude of prayerful dependence upon God, the Greek text suggests faithfulness in attending the congregational gatherings for prayer (she continues in *the* petitions and *the* prayers). Note the order "night and day." This is typically Jewish and reflects the custom of reckoning a day from the sunset of the previous day. The Sabbath began at sundown on Friday.

An excellent example of the ideal Jewish widow was the elderly prophetess Anna who "never left the temple but worshiped night and day, fasting and praying" (Luke 2:36,37). Paul seems to draw upon this ideal as he sketches the requirements which qualify a woman to be a Christian widow.

In contrast is the "pleasure-loving widow" who is "dead even while still alive" (1 Tim. 5:6, *Wey-*

mouth). It may be that Paul is speaking only of self-indulgent widows. Some writers, however, see here an indication that some widows had resorted to prostitution as a means of livelihood. The *Berkeley Version in Modern English* translates "one who lives voluptuously" and *Moffatt* has "the widow who plunges into dissipation." In either case the church would have no responsibility for their welfare.

Pleasure seekers are dead even though they live. They have cut themselves off from the purposes of God which relate to the age to come and have given themselves over to sensual excitement which is very much a part of this present evil age. While existing physically they are dead spiritually. To make pleasure a god is to renounce any claim on the life to come and to "die" to the real life which is fellowship with God through Jesus Christ our Lord. "Now this is eternal life: that they may know you" (John 17:3).

To the various instructions laid out earlier in the letter Timothy is to add these regulations regarding widows. The purpose is that their lives be "free from reproach" (1 Tim. 5:7, *Weymouth*). Like the overseer who must be "above reproach" and "have a good reputation with outsiders" (1 Tim. 3:2,7), the congregation must be careful to give its non-Christian neighbors no occasion for slander. This emphasis reflects the apostle Paul's mature judgment that the faith has the best opportunity for growth and outreach in a social context of stability.

It should go without saying that anyone who will not provide for his relatives (especially his own family) has disowned the faith and is worse off than a pagan (see v. 8). The Greek world had a concept of family responsibility higher than that. To refuse help to a widowed mother would be to sink below the level of morality accepted by pagans. This would be a denial of the faith in the sense that biblical faith must of necessity express itself in acts of loving-kindness. As examples of what God can make out of selfish and self-centered persons, believers are "created in Christ Jesus to do *good works*, which God prepared in advance for us to do" (Eph. 2:10, italics added). As a redeemed people we are to be "eager to do what is good" (Titus 2:14). It would be unthinkable for a Christian not to provide for a needy parent, a denial of the faith. Such a person would be "behaving worse than an unbeliever" *(Weymouth)*.

Paul insists that widows who have children or grandchildren should be cared for by their own families. It would be unfair for the church to carry the burden for these. In fact, if a person does not take care of those within his family who are in need he has denied the faith and is living on a lower level of morality than his pagan neighbors.

Why should the Christian live according to a higher code of ethics than the non-Christian? Is it reasonable to expect that a Christian organization will operate at a higher level of business ethics than a secular organization? From your contacts would you say this is true? Is it also reasonable that the individual Christian live according to a higher standard of ethics than the non-Christian? Is this always the case? Usually the case? Is it the case in your life? It is often true, is it not, that the world holds a higher standard of moral conduct for Christians than believers hold for themselves? Should this be?

What Is a "Congregational Widow?" (5:9,10)

Verses 9 and 10 list three basic requirements for qualifying as a church widow: (1) over sixty, (2) faithful to her husband, and (3) known for good deeds. Several examples are then given for the last requirement.

Writers differ on whether there existed in Paul's time a definite order of widows. Phrases such as "put on the list of widows" (v. 9) and "broken their first pledge" (v. 12) are evidence enough for some to believe that a recognized order of widows (comparable to overseers, 3:1-7, and deacons, 3:8-10,12,13) did in fact exist. Others are not convinced that the church had by that time developed such an office. We do know that by the fourth century widows had become an accepted order in the Christian church. (*The Apostolic Constitutions* is a fourth-century collection of church regulations. Chapters 1-8 of book three deal at length with the order of widows.)

Sixty seems a rather advanced age for becoming a congregational widow. Yet it was widely accepted as the age when a widow's normal passions would weaken, permitting entrance into the final and contemplative period of the life cycle. For reasons to be discussed at a later point (vv. 11-15) Paul held it to be unwise to enroll any widow who had not reached the age of 60.

In the second place a widow must have been "faithful to her husband." This is an exact parallel to the requirement for overseers and deacons (see 3:2,12). There is an ethical requirement for acceptance on the official role of widows. Marital infidelity disqualifies the woman in the same way it does the man.

Some feel that the phrase means "married only once." It is hard to understand, however, why a woman who had lost two husbands by death (not just one) would therefore be any less qualified. Remarriage is not only acceptable but actively urged upon the younger widows (see vv. 11-15). So many of the restrictions under which the church labors are the products of well-intentioned men, but do not represent the mind of God. The legalists of 4:2,3 are examples of this tendency to deny on "religious grounds" what is explicitly approved by God.

The church widow must also be "well-known for her good deeds" (v. 10). That faith must of an inner necessity express itself in a transformed life is never far from Paul's thoughts. Faith, as a mystical relationship unrelated to life, is foreign to New Testament doctrine. Faith is a personal relationship to God which moves the believer irresistibly to do those things God desires. The Christian is under the compulsion of love to do his Master's bidding.

Paul now supplies several examples of what he means by good deeds. "Bringing up children" refers primarily to the normal expectation that a mother supply the physical, emotional, and spiritual needs of her young. It could also refer to the care of orphaned children. In a day when unwanted children were often left unattended to die, unscrupulous persons would sometimes collect them for purposes of slavery and prostitution. Christian love would move the church whenever possible to intervene and make a home for abandoned children. For a woman to help in this ministry of concern would indicate her suitability to be enrolled as a widow.

Widows are to show hospitality. In Paul's day inns were notorious for their immorality. Traveling prophets and teachers would normally stay in the homes of the congregation. Hospitality of this sort ran the risk of putting the believing homeowner at odds with the unbelieving community.

"Washing the feet of the saints" was a menial task necessary in those days because of sandals and dusty roads. We remember how Jesus in the Upper Room removed His outer garment, took a basin of water and washed the feet of the disciples (see John 13:3-11). Then He said, "I have set you an example that you should do as I have done for you" (John 13:15). To be a congregational widow the candidate's "good works" must include the same type of lowly service for others as Jesus had performed.

"Helping those in trouble" is a further indication of commitment to a life of kindly concern. Everyone who in a period of distress has been helped by another knows that "A friend in need is a friend indeed" is far more than a trite slogan.

As a kind of summary statement Paul adds "and has been devoted to all kinds of good works" *(MLB)*. Without commitment there can be no vital Christianity. Frank Laubach has written a book with the title *Channels of Spiritual Power*. The metaphor is taken from the generator installed in a great dam. When water is allowed to enter only the turbine it will soon fill. But when the sluice gates are opened and water is allowed to flow through, then power is generated. So it is with the Christian faith. If we only *hear* the truth we soon become stagnant. Spiritual power is generated when the gates of action are opened and truth understood becomes truth in action.

The first thing that comes to Paul's mind when he wants to illustrate what it means for a widow to be well-known for her good deeds is that she bring up her children properly. Other examples of good deeds are showing hospitality, washing the feet of the saints and helping those in trouble. Note, however, that the woman's role in rearing children comes first.

What is the major responsibility of the contemporary Christian woman? Is her responsibility toward her children any less than it was for her first-century counterpart? Do you think it is likely that a woman can devote considerable time to projects outside the home and not have it affect adversely her role as mother? The feminist movement has

73

gathered significant momentum in recent years. Will this strengthen or weaken the family structure in America? Have you ever heard an impassioned plea for children's rights? Wouldn't it make good sense?

The Special Problems of Young Widows (5:11-16)

The apostle Paul was a remarkable man. Not only was he a learned theologian who could present his case to the intellectuals at Athens (see Acts 17:16-34), but he was also an eminently practical church man who was concerned to spell out proper guidelines for the selection of church widows.

Paul is concerned about the appointment of younger widows (see 1 Tim. 5:11). They are not to be put on the official list. Why not? Because (and here is his straightforward counsel) "when they feel sensuous impulses that alienate them from Christ" (this translation is from the Arndt-Gingrich lexicon, page 420, under the Greek word the King James Version translates "wax wanton") they wish to marry. In 2 Corinthians 11:2 Paul pictures the church as a spiritual bridegroom of Christ. He has promised them "to one husband, to Christ" and desires to present them to him "as a pure virgin." It appears that in some way the church widows had pledged themselves to Christ. In 1 Timothy 5:11 Paul says that dedication to Christ is threatened by "sensual desires." Verse 12 speaks of the judgment that results when the widows "have broken their first pledge." To what extent they may have considered themselves "married" (in a spiritual sense) to Christ is not clear. But it is perfectly clear that subsequent marriage as a result of sensual desire was a violation of their relationship with Christ.

It should be emphasized that Paul does not in any way condemn the natural desires of the widows. What is wrong is the breaking of a pledge. Since

74

physical desire normally continues throughout most of life it is unwise to enter early into an official relationship that closes the door on remarriage. The judgment brought upon widows is the disapproval and censure of the church.

Two additional reasons are given in verse 13 in support of the position that younger widows should not be placed on the official role:

First, *they may "get into the habit of being idle."* A young widow would presumably have more energy and thus be apt to finish her assigned work more quickly, allowing a considerable amount of free time. Paul would agree with the adage, "Idle hands are the devil's workshop." Free time is not wisely spent "going about from house to house."

Second, *idleness lends itself to gossip and meddling.* Scripture is full of warnings about the unwise use of the tongue. Proverbs 6 lists among the seven things which are an abomination to the Lord "a lying tongue . . . a false witness . . . and a man who stirs up dissension among brothers" (vv. 16-19). Ephesians instructs, "Do not let any unwholesome talk come out of your mouths" (4:29). Younger widows with time on their hands would run the danger of unwise speech and "being over-interested in the business of others" *(New Testament in Basic English).* Visitation would provide them with private information which should not be shared with others. This is what Paul intends by the clause "saying things they ought not to."

In view of these considerations it is best for young widows to marry (see 1 Tim. 5:14). This will meet their normal physical needs. They are to have children. God's ideal is the family. Management of the home also falls to them. This kind of domestic responsibility is of far greater benefit to everyone involved than whatever contribution a young woman might make as a congregational widow. Beyond that it gives "the enemy no opportunity for slander." It is impossible to know how many individuals have been turned away from the Christian faith by the shoddy quality of the lives of certain church members. At the same time many have been attracted to Christ by the winsomeness and beauty of the lives of truly committed believers. It *does* make a difference how we live!

The apostle closes the section on younger widows by noting that some "have already played into the enemy's hands" (v. 15, *Phillips*). That is, they have been enrolled as widows far too early in life, and consequently have been subjected to temptations in which they have failed. If turning away to follow Satan (see v. 15) is interpreted in light of sensual desires which overcome dedication to Christ (see v. 11), it may be that Paul intends a reference to prostitution. Because few trades or professions were open to women in that day, a young widow without material support could find herself driven to immorality as a means of livelihood.

As a general principle widows should be provided for by their own next of kin. In this way the church will be able to extend its help for those who are really in need. It is worth noting that early Christian communities were actively concerned about members of their congregation experiencing genuine need. Twentieth-century churches would do well to consider their priorities in light of this example. The percentage of our budget directed toward the physical needs of less fortunate members hardly rivals the amount committed to relatively ornate structures.

Some have puzzled over the meaning of "If any woman who is a believer has widows in her family" in verse 16. Early scribes sensed the problem and offered such corrections as "any believing man" or "any believing man or woman." It is simplest to understand the phrase as referring to a well-off woman in the church in whose household there is a widow (perhaps a mother, mother-in-law, sister, or daughter).

Not only was Paul the greatest theologian of the first century but he was at the same time a remarkably practical man. His profound grasp of the meaning of the Incarnation did not prevent him from giving attention to the more mundane aspects of life. Usually the dreamer and the man of action stand at opposite ends of the spectrum. Paul combined both qualities. His detailed instructions about younger widows shows his concern for every part of congregational life.

How would you classify yourself? Are you philosophically inclined, concerned primarily with the central issues of life and society, or are you the practical sort who would rather act than spin your wheels thinking? What are the particular problems of the idealist (the dreamer)? What about Mr. Practical himself? If part of Paul's usefulness lay in the breadth of his personality, do you think it would be wise for each of us to work toward the development of that side of our temperament which is less dominant? Or has God made us what we are, personality-wise, and should we let it go at that?

Now Concerning Elders (5:17-25)

The Jewish synagogue was administered by a board of elders. The term does not require that we necessarily think of elders as elderly men, although most social institutions tend to be under the direction of mature men. The early Christian congregation quite naturally borrowed their organizational pattern from Judaism. Christian elders played more or less the same institutional role as did their Jewish counterparts.

Paul says that elders who carry out their responsibilities effectively are "worthy of double honor" (v. 17). There is no doubt that financial remuneration is what the apostle is talking about. But what does he mean by a "double stipend" *(NEB)*? *Williams* has the interesting translation, "considered as deserving twice the salary they get."

It seems that a distinction is beginning to appear between elders who have general oversight and others who have taken up more specific and time-consuming activities on behalf of the church. One special example would be "those whose work is preaching and teaching." While elders probably held down regular jobs, some gave so much of their time to the church that it was appropriate to pay them a stipend. For those who directed well the affairs of the church, double payment was in order. It is helpful to keep in mind that we are not talking about full-time ministry. To put it in modern terms, Paul is not saying that if the base salary of ordinary church workers is $10,000 per year, those who do a good job should get $20,000. It is quite possible that by "double honor" Paul intends nothing more than an ample salary.

Note the centrality of "preaching and teaching." The Christian church centers on the proclamation of the gospel and the teaching of its implications for theology and ethics. Elders who "work hard at their preaching and teaching" *(NASB)* are worthy of generous material support from those who benefit from their toil. In 3:3 we learned that an elder must be no "lover of money." This does not imply that he is to become the resident pauper of the congregation. He is worthy of adequate and generous support. Laymen who pray for their pastor, "Lord, you keep him humble, and we'll keep him poor," are out of step with the biblical position.

Paul supports his admonition with two citations from Scripture. The first is from Deuteronomy 25:4, "Do not muzzle an ox while it is treading out the grain." In ancient days grain was separated by driving oxen over sheaves laid out on a threshing floor. The oxen were not to be muzzled so that from time to time they could eat of the grain. In 1 Corinthians 9:9 Paul quotes the same verse and goes on to show God's concern that those who have sown "spiritual seed" should "reap a material harvest" (v. 11).

To the Old Testament citation Paul adds the words of Jesus, "The worker deserves his wages" (Luke 10:7). (This quote would seem to date 1 Timothy after the Gospel—and therefore in the 70s or 80s—except that it could just as easily come from an earlier source available to Luke.) The important thing is that Paul designates the words of Jesus as "Scripture." To the Old Testament, already accepted as the Word of God, is now added the teaching of Jesus.

The point is that elders, hard at work in the ministry of the church, are fully deserving of adequate financial support from the congregation.

Turning to a related subject Paul tells Timothy not to consider any charge leveled against an elder unless it is confirmed by two or three witnesses (see 1 Tim. 5:19). Once again the principle stems from Jewish legal procedure (see Deut. 19:15). It was followed throughout the apostolic church (see 2 Cor. 13:1). This kind of protection against slander was rather unusual in ancient times. It assumes that accusations are more easily made than proven. If the same principle were followed in normal relationships, rumor would die for lack of support. The ease with which we accept hearsay reveals more about our own weak-nesses than about the person placed in question.

Elders who continue in sin, however, are to be rebuked publicly (see 1 Tim. 5:20). If accusations are found to be true and private consultation brings about no change (see Matt. 18:16), the elder is to be rebuked before the entire congregation. This will serve as a warning to others, both the elders and members of the congregation. Church discipline is rarely exercised in the modern church. And when it is, it is often carried out in a stern and loveless fashion. The ideal is concern both for the individual who has sinned and for the congregation affected by his waywardness. Firm yet gentle is still the best approach.

At this point Paul delivers a charge to Timothy in an extraordinarily serious manner. "I solemnly command you" (v. 21) is the way *The Living Bible* translates the verb. The same word is used of the rich man in hell who pleads that Lazarus the beggar *warn* his brothers about the place of torment (see Luke 16:28). The charge to Timothy is given "in the sight of God and Christ Jesus and the elect angels." All will be involved in final judgment (see Matt. 25:31; Rev. 14:10) so it is appropriate that their presence be invoked at this moment.

The instructions that Timothy is to keep without partiality include not only the matter of how to handle accusations against elders but the preceding rules governing the appointment of congregational widows. In both cases it is extremely important that no favoritism be shown. Elders are to be treated alike and widows must be handled with all fairness. Anyone charged with responsibility over the welfare of others should be acutely aware of the absolute necessity of fairness. Nothing divides a group more quickly than favoritism. Paul says that it is crucial that

Timothy be aware of this potential trouble.

The seriousness of judgment following the misconduct of an elder leads Paul to warn Timothy, "Do not be hasty in the laying on of hands" (v. 22). The reference is to the ordination of elders. Competent men who have proven themselves absolutely trustworthy are the only ones who should be considered for church leadership (see 3:1-16). Decisions must not be made hastily. Should Timothy ordain an unworthy candidate he would be sharing "in the sins of others." That is, by approving of a questionable candidate he would necessarily share responsibility for the results of his failure. *Knox* translates, "And so share the blame for the sins of others." In carrying out his charge Timothy is to "keep [himself] clear of fault."

Paul's advice on taking a little wine for medicinal purposes (v. 23) should be understood in light of two considerations:

First, it appears that Timothy *had decided in favor of total abstinence.* There was an ascetic tradition in Judaism. For example, the Nazirite vow prohibited not only wine and strong drink, but also the eating of "grapes or raisins" (Num. 6:3). Timothy's mother was Jewish (see Acts 16:1) but his father was Greek. Gnosticism (a Greek philosophy) had its followers who taught that the body should be severely held in check (see 1 Tim. 4:1-3). These influences could have led Timothy to decide against wine of any sort.

Second, Timothy appears to *have enjoyed less than adequate health.* Since wine was widely used in antiquity for medicinal purposes Paul counsels Timothy to take a little wine "for the good of your stomach and your recurring illness" *(MLB).* It will aid digestion and "help you to get over your frequent spells of illness" *(Phillips).*

It should be noted that Paul's advice has nothing

to do with what is currently called "social drinking." It was given in a cultural context in which wine was served as a safeguard against impure water and as a beneficial tonic for certain digestive problems.

The remark about wine should be taken as a parenthetical statement. The last two verses of the chapter continue the discussion on the appointment of elders. Since first impressions can be misleading, Timothy is not to move ahead too quickly with the laying on of hands.

"The sins of some men are obvious" (v. 24). It is evident that judgment awaits them. The sins of others, however, "trail behind them." That is, they come to light at a later time. The judgment Paul speaks of is final judgment. Jesus taught that "there is nothing concealed that will not be disclosed, or hidden that will not be made known" (Luke 12:2). The day will come when "God will judge men's secrets" (Rom. 2:16).

In the same way some good deeds are immediately apparent and others will be revealed later. In appointing elders it is wise to take one's time in that the real quality of their lives may not show up at first. Impulsive decisions based on first impressions are unwise. Better to test the candidate over a period of time (see 1 Tim. 3:10).

For some Christians the question of wine has loomed large. Adults who have come to Christ out of a background of mild social drinking have often had to deal with the question after some period of time spent within the Christian church. Depending upon the specific group we find various answers to the question, Is drinking wine permissible for the Christian believer? Paul's word to Timothy encouraging him to take a little wine for his stomach's sake (see 1 Tim. 5:23) normally enters the discussion.

Why do you think Timothy had to be encouraged to take a little wine? How often is wine used today for medicinal purposes? Is there anything inherently wrong with wine? Why is drunkenness wrong? Is restrained and moderate use of wine permissible for Christians? What factors are present in contemporary culture that were absent in first-century culture and affect our evaluation of the wisdom of Christians using wine? Do you know of any radiant Spirit-filled Christians who also publicly use wine? How does the biblical principle of not causing our brother to stumble (1 Cor. 8—10) relate to the question of wine in the life of believers? What about Romans 14:23?

6

FIRST TIMOTHY SIX

How to Be a Christian Slave (6:1,2b)

Slavery was a prominent and accepted part of ancient civilization. It is said that there were some 60 million slaves in the Roman empire alone. Masters exercised the power of life and death over their human property. The vast majority of slaves existed as domestic animals. The entire social system was grossly unjust. Slavery was an expression of the darker side of human nature.

Some have wondered why Paul didn't speak out against slavery. Was he less concerned about this injustice than modern civil rights workers are?

An answer lies along the following lines. Early Christianity was convinced that the Lord would return in the near future. Better to spend one's time in telling the good news than attempting the reform of a deeply ingrained social custom. To urge a rebellion at that point in social history would have risked the lives of thousands of slaves and have diverted the energies of the church from its major priority.

It should be noted that Christianity by no means failed to make an impact upon the institution of slavery. It has been the major social force in altering man's understanding of the worth of the individual. Before God, all men are of equal value. This realization leads to the overthrow of slavery as a social institution.

In verse 1 Paul instructs Christian slaves to "treat their masters with the greatest respect" *(Goodspeed)*. The temptation to look down on a non-Christian master, especially if he were harsh or cruel, would naturally be strong to a Christian slave who had found new worth and self-respect in his relationship to Christ. It was important, however, that the church give no occasion for pagans to slander the name of God and the teachings of the faith. Respect from outsiders was a major principle in Paul's ordering of the church (see 3:2,7).

Verse 2 deals specifically with Christian slaves who had believing masters. In this case it would be relatively easy for slaves to take unwarranted liberties with their masters. Since they were in fact brothers in Christ the social distance would tend to dissolve. Familiarity can breed contempt, or at least "less respect." A Christian slave should serve his believing master even better because of the brotherly love that exists between them in view of their oneness in Christ.

Although slavery as a formal institution no longer exists in enlightened countries, Paul's advice on the conduct and attitude of slaves has relevance for us today. In our contemporary social relationships we still work within various kinds of accepted hierarchies. A modern expression of Paul's basic principle would be that believers employed by others should consider their supervisors as worthy of respect. A negative and carping attitude alienates the non-Christian from the one source of spiritual help. Christians should always outdo unbelievers in anything they attempt. This should especially be the case when both employer and employee are children of God and brothers in Christ.

Paul appears to accept the institution of slavery; at least he counsels slaves to show respect to their masters. This lack of opposition to slavery on Paul's part has caused many modern writers to criticize the apostle for lack of social concern.

Do you think that Paul approved of some men owning other men? Why didn't Paul get involved in an abolitionist movement? If Paul were alive today do you think he would be for or against the civil rights movement to end discrimination against minority groups? Would he give up preaching the gospel in order to devote himself full-time to the task of bringing about social equality in modern society? How much time and energy should today's evangelical give to issues of social justice?

An Exposé of False Teachers (6:2c-5)

The last sentence of verse 2 belongs with the paragraph that follows. The *New International Version* has unfortunately added (without manuscript evidence) the words "on them." This would relate the exhortation to the preceding paragraph on slaves. The Greek text says very simply, "These things teach and exhort." It introduces the concluding section of the epistle. From this point on Paul treats one subject after another in fairly rapid sequence. Some are related, others are not.

The first paragraph deals with false teachers. Paul has some rather scathing words to say about a false teacher. He is a "pompous ignoramus" (v. 4, *NEB*) with "a morbid craving for speculations and arguments" *(Goodspeed)*. Their activity results in all sorts of slander and strife. False teachers are in it because they "think religion is a way to make money" (v. 5, *Beck*). Not a pretty picture!

False doctrine is teaching that "does not agree to the sound instruction of our Lord Jesus Christ and to godly teaching" (v. 3). Note how central the teaching of Jesus was in the life of the early church. In another letter Paul went out of his way to point out that what he was about to say at that point was *not* a command from the Lord (see 1 Cor. 7:25). This argues a strong reliance of Paul upon the teaching of Jesus where exceptions are not noted. From John 21:25 we understand that the work and words of Jesus were far more extensive than what was recorded in the Gospels.

The instruction of Jesus is "sound" (1 Tim. 6:3), that is, wholesome or healthy. The word is used of physical health in Jesus' statement, "It is not the *healthy* who need a doctor" (Luke 5:31, italics added). Christian doctrine brings health to those who are sick with the virus of sin. It restores the one who believes to the kind of spiritual health intended by God.

The false teacher is said to be conceited and without understanding. There is nothing quite like the lack of knowledge to produce a bloated opinion of oneself. True knowledge humbles. It was Edison who said that we don't yet know the millionth part of anything.

Most writers feel that the false teachers who were infiltrating the early church were related in some way to the professional orators, or sophists, who made their living by pleasing large crowds with their clever use of language and by teaching others how to speak and argue cleverly. They were marked by conceit, useless controversy, and the love of money. Some apparently saw the Christian faith as an opportunity to ply their trade for a handsome reward.

87

In contrast to the "sound instruction" of the apostle, the false teachers have "an *unhealthy* interest in controversies and arguments" (1 Tim. 6:4 italics added). In rejecting truth for error they reveal how sick they are. The results are predictable. *Phillips* lists the first four as "jealousy, quarreling, insults and malicious innuendoes." These are self-explanatory! As we might expect they are followed by "constant friction" (v. 5). Such activity left the church in a state of disarray.

The false teachers are described further in three ways:

First, they are men of *corrupt minds.* Their entire outlook (not simply their reasoning powers) is degraded. In Acts 2:27 the word is used of physical decay. It is equally possible for the mind to "rot." Second, they have "*lost all hold on the Truth*" *(TCNT). The New International Version* implies that *they* are the victims ("robbed of the truth"), but the opposite is true. They are the ones who have repudiated the truth. Third, they think that "*godliness is a means to financial gain.*" Obviously, they are not concerned with true godliness. They are interested only in a "godliness" that gives them access to the church for the purpose of making money.

The *Didache* is a second-century manual on Christian morals and church practices. At one point it notes that if an apostle asks for money he is a false apostle (xi. 6). Apparently the Christian congregation was a relatively easy target for those who wanted to make a fast buck. Ephesus had its spiritual mercenaries who had figured out that godliness is a means to financial gain (see v. 6).

To what extent do some people today associate themselves with religious organizations for the financial advantage it may bring to them? What professions might be particularly susceptible to this temptation? Which services in the church should be rewarded with financial payment? Preaching? Teaching? Music? Maintenance? Nursery care? How should we go about determining what we should pay for and what we might expect on a voluntary basis?

A Word About Money (6:6-10)

The false teachers thought of godliness as a means of financial gain. Paul taught that godliness (in the truest sense) *is* a great gain, specifically when it is accompanied by a contented spirit. The requirement of contentment rules out the self-seeking concern of the financially motivated and moves the entire discussion onto a higher plane. Verse 6 enshrines a great truth. A godly life which exhibits deep personal satisfaction is richly rewarding. It is "great gain."

Three hundred years before Christ a Greek philosopher, Epicurus, said, "Give me a barley cake and a glass of water and I am ready to rival Zeus for happiness." The deceitful nature of material things has been widely recognized. Upon learning that he had lost everything, the venerable Job confessed, "Naked I came from my mother's womb, and naked I will depart" (Job 1:21; see Eccl. 5:15). Paul now echoes the same sentiment. "We brought nothing into the world, and we can take nothing out of it." The Spanish proverb has it, "There are no pockets in a shroud."

Both birth and death are lonely experiences. We enter this life with nothing except potential. We leave this life with nothing except a character (and destiny) determined by how we have used that potential. How sad that by nature men pursue that which can never give satisfaction. Instead of loving people and using things the usual pattern is to love things and use

89

people. Huston Smith observes that we can never get enough of what we really do not want.

Food and clothing, the basic requirements of life, are all we need. The second half of verse 8 may be taken as an exhortation, "Let us be content with these" *(MLB)*. Those who set their hearts on becoming wealthy subject themselves to great temptation. They walk into a trap and "become the prey of many foolish and harmful ambitions" (v. 9, *TCNT*). They "plunge men into ruin and destruction." Notice the progression: first they desire to be rich; then they are trapped by their own lust; finally they are dragged down to moral destruction. James, likewise, speaks of desire giving birth to sin which leads to death (see Jas. 1:15).

The idea expressed in the proverbial saying, "The love of money is a root of all kinds of evil," was widely known and accepted. A Greek writer of the sixth century B.C. (Phocylides of Miletus) wrote, "The love of money is the mother of all evils." Paul's maxim is frequently misquoted or misapplied. It does not say that *money* is the root of evil. Money in itself is morally neutral. Whether it leads to evil or good depends entirely on how it is used. Neither does it say that the love of money is the single cause of all evil. What it does say, as *Phillips* puts it, is that "loving money leads to all kinds of evil" (v. 10). The love of money (all that it can buy and do) had lured the false teachers into all sorts of foolish and wicked desires (see v. 9). It remains even today as a primary reason for failure in life. Even though men know better they pursue happiness through possessions.

The end result is pitiful. Craving after money, people wander from the faith. Jesus said, "You cannot serve both God and Money" (Matt. 6:24). In pursuing gain the false teachers necessarily turned away from God. The result of their apostasy was that they "pierced themselves with many griefs" (1 Tim. 6:10). The pursuit of pleasure ends with the pangs of remorse. The enticements of evil result ironically in their opposites. The desire to possess stifles the ability to enjoy. Sin is by nature self-defeating. Its path is strewn with disappointment and disillusionment.

The New Testament has much to say about the folly of pursuing money and what it is supposed to be able to buy. The successful farmer of Luke 12 who calculated that by building bigger barns in which to store his crops he would be able to live out his years with security and pleasure was called a "fool" by God. That very night was to be his last and his wealth would go to others (see Luke 12:16-20). Paul's warning is well-known—"The love of money is a root of all kinds of evil."

Why do you think the New Testament has so much to say about the pursuit of money? Do the poor "love money" or is that only a problem of the rich? Why do you think God allows some Christians to be well-off financially? If a rich believer has paid his tithe is he then free to use the other 90 percent as he pleases? Should the poor believer be excused from a tithe because he doesn't have very much? What do you think of the idea of Christian parents leaving the bulk of their inheritance to worthy causes if their own children are reasonably well-off financially?

Here Are Your Orders, Timothy (6:11-16)

In many ways this paragraph is the high point of Paul's letter. It begins with a personal charge to his young colleague Timothy and ends in a magnificent doxology. In contemporary idiom one could say that this is "the best of Paul."

Timothy is addressed as "man of God." He is

God's man to carry out God's will at that time and in that place. The term is common in the Old Testament as a designation for men such as Moses (see Deut. 33:1), Elijah (see 1 Kings 17:18) and others. Timothy stands in a long line of men chosen by God to carry out His redemptive plan in history.

Timothy is counseled to flee from all the evils which characterize the life-style of the false teachers. "But you, man of God" implies a strong contrast. Instead he is to strive constantly after those virtues which are especially appropriate for his pastoral role. "Righteousness" and "godliness" are to be taken in a general sense as describing conduct that is upright and pious. "Faith" and "love" are the fundamental Christian virtues. "Endurance" is not patience in the passive sense of quiet acceptance but steadfastness in the positive sense of "masculine constancy under trial" (Barclay).

Paul is fond of metaphors taken from athletic games. "Run the great race of the Faith" (v. 12) is how one translation *(TCNT)* paraphrases "fight the good fight." The Greek text suggests a continuing contest. The "fight of the faith" has nothing to do with any difficulty in believing. It refers to the difficulties that result from living for God in a secular and hostile world.

Timothy is to "take hold of the eternal life" not only because God has called him to this, but also because he openly confessed it before many witnesses. Eternal life is pictured as the prize for winning the race. If the picture of a runner striving to win so as to gain a medal serves to suggest a way of salvation not quite in keeping with the Pauline doctrine of righteousness apart from works, it should be noted that we are dealing with a metaphor or analogy whose controlling purpose is to place the truth in a new perspective, not to provide a theological declaration.

Timothy's "good confession in the presence of many witnesses" is a reference to his confession of faith made at the time of his baptism. It is compared with the "good confession" made by Christ before (or in the time of) Pontius Pilate. *Goodspeed's* translation of verse 13, "Who in testifying before Pontius Pilate made his great confession," understands as background Jesus' reply to Pilate's question, "Are you the king of the Jews?" Jesus answered, "Yes, it is as you say" (Luke 23:3). The term may be more general and refer to Jesus' fidelity to the truth as revealed by God and now contained within the basic Christian confession of faith.

It is possible that an early creed lies behind the two elements reflected in 1 Timothy 6:13. God is portrayed as the one "who gives life to everything." In the Apostles' Creed we acknowledge our belief in "God the Father, maker of heaven and earth." He is the source of all creation and especially the author of life. Jesus is portrayed as making a noble confession in the time of Pontius Pilate. Fidelity to truth and obedience to God took Him through the experience of the cross to the victory of the Resurrection. The death, burial and resurrection of Jesus Christ is the second great element in the Apostles' Creed.

Timothy is to "keep this commandment without spot or blame" (v. 14). The commandment is not the earlier admonition to "fight the good fight" (v. 12) but is the total responsibility to maintain fidelity to the Christian revelation and all it implies for life and conduct. To keep it "without spot or blame" means to keep it free from the contaminating effects of heresy and idle speculation. Truth is threatened by error. It is Timothy's job to see that the truth of the gospel is not compromised by the devious doctrines of the false teachers. There will come a time when such a task will no longer be necessary—that is, at "the appearing of our Lord Jesus Christ." Since the charge is given in the first place to a young minister living in the middle of the first century, it appears that Paul, here as elsewhere (1 Thess. 4:17, "*we* who are still alive"), expected the second coming of Christ within his (or Timothy's) lifetime. This great epiphany (the Greek is *epiphaneia*) or appearance of Christ will come about in God's own time. In Scripture the time of the end is always presented as determined solely by God. According to Mark 13:32 neither the angels nor the Son know the hour or the day.

The very mention of the glorious return of Christ and God's sovereign act of closing the book of human history moves Paul to give voice to one of the most exalted doxologies in all of Scripture. Whether or not the phrases reflect "the devotional treasury of the Hellenistic synagogue" (Kelly) or perhaps an early Christian hymn, is of no great significance. What is important is to catch the apostle's exalted vision of God as supreme Ruler of the entire created order, the source of all life, so awesome in splendor that no one can approach or even see Him.

God is blessed in that He enjoys within Himself the perfection of every virtue and attribute appropriate to His nature. He is absolutely sovereign in His control over the created order. Nothing lies beyond His power. He is "King of kings and Lord of lords" (1 Tim. 6:15). (For Jewish parallels see Deut. 10:17; 2 Mac. 13:4, *Apoc.* The same dual title is ascribed to Christ in Rev. 17:14; 19:16.) He rules over all rulers and is exalted above every earthly sovereign. It appears that John has in mind the claims of Roman rulers who considered themselves supreme.

God alone is immortal (see 1 Tim. 6:16). Although

believers are "immortal" in the sense of having received eternal life, God is uniquely immortal in that He Himself is the source of that life. He is not subject to the aging process of time. He is immune from death.

God lives in "unapproachable light." When God spoke from the burning bush Moses hid his face (Exod. 3:2-6). He is the one "whom no mortal eye has ever seen" (1 Tim. 6:16, *Phillips;* see Exod. 33:20; John 1:18). In theological terms, He is transcendent and invisible. The doxology ends with the ascription to God of "honor and eternal dominion" *(NASB).* He is worthy of praise and power forever. "Amen," so let it be, writes Paul.

The contemporary church is in need of a view of God that stresses His greatness and transcendent power. Modern hymns often bring Him down to our level of drab familiarity. He becomes the panacea for trivial ills, the support for our lackluster programs. We forget the awesome quality of His divine nature. To meditate on Paul's great doxology is to realize again the greatness of God and the wonder of His eternal plan.

Paul had an exalted view of God. God alone is sovereign. He rules over all earthly kings and authorities. He possesses within Himself immortality. He is beyond the reach of death and decay. He stands outside the created order which is gradually running down. He lives in the midst of such splendor that the natural eye cannot see Him.

What is your view of God? In our churches do we treat God as God or have we come to think of Him in terms of a good-natured but relatively helpless friend? To what extent do our hymns portray God as less sovereign and powerful than He is? Is the love of God as popularly perceived in our churches more like sentimental benevolence than strong and courageous redemptive activity? J.B. Phillips wrote a book titled *Your God Is Too Small.* Is He?

Advice to the Wealthy (6:17-19)

Paul now returns to the subject of money. Earlier (see vv. 3-10) he was speaking of those who desired to be rich: now he addresses himself to those who *are* rich. Note that their wealth is "in this present world." It has no necessary bearing on the world to come. It relates only to the few short years we call life and is without significance for the endless ages which await.

The rich are to be warned about two attitudes to which they are especially prone:

First, the rich are *not to be arrogant.* Possessing wealth tends to give a sense of superiority. The rich often consider those who have not made it financially as intrinsically inferior. This seems to be especially true of those who have come by wealth through no particular effort of their own.

Second, the rich are *not to put their hope in wealth* because it is so uncertain. Fortunes may be lost as well as gained. In any case, wealth is deceptive because it cannot purchase those things which truly satisfy. In contrast, the rich are to set their hope on God. It is God who "richly provides us with everything for our enjoyment." This remarkable promise echoes the substance of the psalmist's words, "Delight yourself in the Lord and he will give you the desires of your heart" (Ps. 37:4). And again, "In Thy right hand there are pleasures forever" (Ps. 16:11, *NASB*). One of the most deceptive lies in Satan's arsenal is that God calls us away from pleasure and subjects us to a drab and colorless life. At Ephesus the lie was propagated by the false teachers who forbade marriage and certain foods (see 1 Tim. 4:3). The only things that God forbids are those which, if pursued, will ultimately diminish joy. His way is the way of abundant life (see John 10:10).

The rich are to use their wealth for the benefit of others. They are to be "rich in good deeds . . . generous and willing to share" (1 Tim. 6:18). For the believer, money is a trust. God does not intend it to be squandered on personal and material luxuries. The well-to-do Christian has the unique opportunity of using his means for the nurture of the church and the spread of the gospel. He is subject, however, to the special temptation of spending it on himself. While we may doubt the economic soundness of the early church's experiment in communal living, we cannot for a minute deny that their sharing of all things (see Acts 4:32,33) was anything but a proper expression of Christian love. By their generosity the rich will be laying up treasure for themselves and so build a solid foundation for the coming age. In helping others they are actually helping themselves. It is one of the great paradoxes of Christian living that what we keep we lose and what we give we retain. By sharing their abundance the rich will "gain the only true life" *(TCNT)*.

It will be helpful to think for a moment about Paul's statement that God is one who "richly provides us with everything for our enjoyment" (v. 17). *Moffatt* translates, "Who richly provides us with all the joys of life." This is an amazing assertion. It runs counter to all those views of God that mistakenly portray Him as a morbidly serious potentate whose grim hold on the world squeezes out any vestige of pleasure.

Do you think that the average church today thinks of God as concerned about the believer's enjoyment? Does God experience pleasure? Should Christians "get a kick" out of life? When does pleasure become sinful? Does sin bring pleasure? Does it promise pleasure? Does enjoyment of life necessarily rule out concern for the missions of the church? What do you think of the view expressed by the Westminster Confession that "the chief end of man is to glorify God and enjoy him forever"?

A Last Word (6:20,21)

The name Timothy means "one who honors God." By using the name in direct address (in reading v. 20 put a long pause after "Timothy") Paul may be stressing the necessity that Timothy live up to his name in carrying out his responsibility toward the church at Ephesus. Specifically, he is to "guard what has been entrusted to [his] care." The deposit or trust that Timothy is to guard is that essential body of Christian truth by which the church came to be and continues to grow. As a trust it is to be maintained without change. Thus Timothy is to "turn a deaf ear to empty and worldly chatter" *(NEB)*. Once again we are warned against wasting time and energy in futile debate with would-be religious intellectuals who have become enamored with rhetoric and wandered from the truth.

"The opposing ideas of what is falsely called knowledge" (6:20) translates an interesting phrase in the original. The Greek word *antithesis* is carried over directly into English to mean "a rhetorical contrast of ideas." A famous second-century heretic by the name of Marcion wrote a book called *Antitheses* in which he claimed that there were a number of contradictions between the Old Testament and the Gospels. The "oppositions" or antitheses to which Paul refers are the counter-affirmations proposed by the false teachers on the basis of pseudo-knowledge and set over against the sound doctrines of the Christian faith. Those that claim to possess this knowledge have missed the mark and gone astray from the faith.

How appropriate that Paul should close his letter with a reference to grace (see v. 21). It is the grace of God—His unmerited favor toward the undeserving—that stands at the heart of all of Paul's teaching. Man has sinned and incurred the wrath of God. Yet God poured out His love for man in providing salvation. He is a God of grace. His gracious acts give expression to love as the essential attribute of His being.

One final note. The last word in the letter ("you") is plural in Greek. Why would Paul expand his brief benediction so as to include others since the letter is written to Timothy? Probably because what appears to have been written as a personal letter to the pastor was in fact intended to be read to the entire congregation (see Col. 4:16).

The church at Ephesus had its self-appointed intellectuals who took great delight in high-sounding words and any secular insight that seemed to undermine the Christian faith. The *New English Bible* translates, "Turn a deaf ear to empty and worldly chatter and the contradictions of so-called 'knowledge'" (1 Tim. 6:20). Truth and error have from the beginning been locked in mortal combat. Error has enjoyed the advantages of deceitful rhetoric and (all too often) the "consensus of scholarly opinion."

Why is it that error seems to find a more ready audience than truth? Do unregenerate men want to know the truth about themselves? Do most seekers after truth actually seek after truth? Is truth simple or complex? Is empirical truth (truth arrived at by scientific experimentation) different from revealed truth (truth from Scripture)? Is all truth one? Is there any possibility that science will ever disprove Scripture?

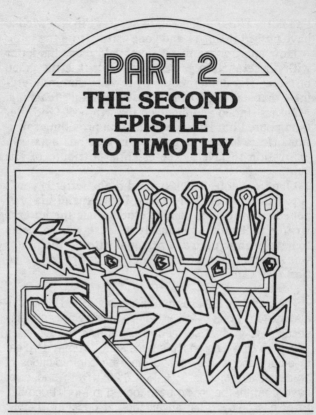

PART 2
THE SECOND EPISTLE TO TIMOTHY

Second Timothy is the last letter we know of which was written by the apostle Paul. He wrote it from a Roman prison (1:8; 2:9) shortly before he was put to death (4:6-8). (The letter to Titus was written from Nicopolis in Greece [Titus 3:12] and belongs chronologically between the two letters to Timothy.) It is in a sense the last will and testament of the greatest missionary-theologian of early Christianity.

7

SECOND TIMOTHY ONE

Some Opening Words (1:1,2)

Like all Paul's letters, except Philippians and the two Thessalonian epistles, 2 Timothy begins with a declaration of Paul's apostleship. It was supremely important to Paul that he had been chosen and sent out on a mission (that is what "apostle" means) by the will of God. He had not chosen the task. God had determined that this would be his role. Paul's mission was to proclaim the promise of life that is found in Christ Jesus. In essence this life is fellowship with the resurrected and exalted Son of God. It begins here and now when a person invites Christ into his life but its fullness awaits that glorious moment when time gives way to eternity and sin is forever removed. It is then that we will fully grasp what it means to be "in Christ Jesus" (v. 1).

Paul writes to "Timothy, my dear son" (v. 2). A strong bond of affection existed between the veteran apostle and his young helper. As a spiritual father Paul was concerned for his "son" whom he had left in Ephesus with the difficult task of managing a church infiltrated by false teachers. Paul's premonition of his approaching execution adds a note of urgency to the entire letter.

The formal apostolic blessing in verse 2 parallels exactly its counterpart in 1 Timothy 1:2. Some have wondered why Paul would begin a letter to a close friend and helper in such a formal way. The answer undoubtedly is that he intended the letter not only for Timothy but for the entire congregation as well. That is the best explanation of the plural in the final clause of both letters—"Grace be with you all" (1 Tim. 6:21; 2 Tim. 4:22).

Paul calls Timothy his "dear son." They had shared many rich experiences in the years they worked together in the missionary outreach of the early church. They had faced danger together. A deep bond of affection had developed between the apostle and his companion.

What opportunity exists in the modern church for deep friendships to develop? Do you think the closeness of our fellowship is directly related to the extent of our shared experiences? If so, what does this suggest about the kind of activities a church should plan for its members? Why is drinking coffee together less effective for building meaningful relationships than an activity such as calling together on a needy family for the purpose of giving material help?

How I Long to See You, Timothy! (1:3-5)

So many of Paul's letters begin with thanksgiving. A continuing awareness of the grace and goodness of God will of necessity move the believer to express his gratitude. It would appear that much of our ill humor results from inadequate exposure to the greatness of God. Unmoved by the wonder of His grace we gripe our way through life. Not so Paul. Loving service leaves little time for complaining.

Paul says that he serves God, as did his forebearers, with a clear conscience. He takes pride in the religious heritage which is his by virtue of his Jewish nationality. His service is carried out without the slightest doubt that this is exactly what God has called him to. A clear (or clean—the word is *katharos*, compare the English "catharsis") conscience is absolutely essential in Christian service. To live under guilt is to deny the message we proclaim.

Night and day (note the Jewish order) Paul remembers Timothy without ceasing in his prayers. Throughout his letters Paul counsels believers to pray. "Pray continually," he challenges the congregation at Thessalonica (1 Thess. 5:17). Here is evidence that he practiced what he preached. He knew that the real adversaries of the gospel were supernatural malignant beings (see Eph. 6:12). This demands that God Himself enter into the conflicts of life. Only by prayer can the "great evil princes of darkness who rule this world" (Eph. 6:12, *TLB*) be put to rout.

In ancient days and especially in eastern lands men were less apt to stifle their emotions. Paul remembers the tears that Timothy shed when they parted. Now he yearns (the verb is intense) to see him again so that he may be filled with joy (see 2 Tim. 1:4). Tears and joy belong very much together.

We do not know what may have at that moment prompted the memory of Timothy's sincere faith. Some suggest that Paul could have just received some news about his fellow worker. It is equally possible (and more probable) that while praying for Timothy Paul's thoughts focused on his young helper's genuine faith in God.

Timothy had one great advantage—both his

mother and grandmother were believing Christians (see v. 5). In Acts 16:1 his mother is said to be "a Jewess and a believer." In the same passage we learn that his father was a Greek. Since there is no mention of his father at this point in Paul's letter it would appear that he was a nonbeliever. The reference to Lois the grandmother as well as Eunice the mother does not argue three successive generations in a Christian family. It appears that they were the first two persons in Timothy's family to come to faith in Christ. Paul is convinced that this same faith now lives in Timothy.

The world has yet to see a person who has made a profound spiritual impact on his generation who was not a man of prayer. Not only does prayer change things but without prayer nothing changes. The New Testament presents Paul as a tremendous activist. He was always on his way somewhere. He is inevitably involved in the proclamation of the gospel and all the many activities connected with such a mission. Yet night and day he remembers his fellow workers in prayer.

How great do you think is the temptation to leave God out of your plans? In your experience have you found that prayer is the dynamic center of all Christian activity? Jesus said, "Apart from me you can do nothing" (John 15:5). To what extent do we really believe that? Would our lives be more fruitful if we took prayer more seriously?

Rekindle the Flame (1:6,7)

Because Paul is certain that Timothy is a man of genuine faith he now charges him to "fan into flame the gift of God" (v. 6). In his earlier letter Paul had written of the gift which was bestowed on Timothy at his ordination (see 1 Tim. 4:14). Here he specifically says that it was through the laying on of his (Paul's) hands that the *charisma*, the spiritual gift or endowment, came to Timothy.

The gift is pictured as a fire that needs to be stirred up in order that its flame be kept burning brightly. God's gifts are distributed by His Spirit as He wills. Man has no part in "lighting the fire" (to borrow Paul's metaphor). The gifts are kept at full flame, however, by the activity of man. There is nothing automatic about the gifts that would exclude man's involvement. Spiritual gifts are not the same as natural abilities. While they may relate to such abilities, they are *spiritual* endowments provided by God for the building and strengthening of Christian congregations.

It is right that Timothy should fan into flame his spiritual gift because he did not receive from God a "spirit of timidity" (v. 7). Apparently the young minister was rather demure and had shied away from exercising the authority that went with his role as leader of the church. The word "timidity" actually means "cowardice." In Mark 4:40 Jesus says to His terrified disciples, "Why are you such cowards?" *(NEB)*, a different form of the same word. Leadership requires the moral courage to face unpleasant situations and take appropriate action. It is worth noting that Paul includes himself ("did not give *us*") in the exhortation, probably to soften the blow.

The spirit that they received is described in three ways:

First, it is a *spirit of power*. This does not imply authoritarianism. It is rather the moral courage that enables a person to take a bold stand for what is right. It is the power that flows from the exercise of strong convictions.

Second, is also the *spirit of love*. Only if love is thought of as weak sentiment or passive acceptance is there any tension between power and love. As defined by the cross, love is a strong and virile act of the will on behalf of the welfare of others.

Third, it is a *spirit of self-discipline* or personal restraint. That a person must be able to rule himself in order to rule others has long been acknowledged. When God chooses a man to govern the church He supplies him with the power to govern himself as well. Whether he uses that power depends upon how faithfully he exercises his gift.

Throughout the two letters Paul counsels his young colleague to take command of his responsibilities. It appears that Timothy was a bit retiring and somewhat timid. Paul reminds him that God does not give His workmen a spirit of timidity but a spirit of power.

Do you think the church today is too timid in its presentation of the claims of Christ? Are we overly concerned about whether Christian standards will offend the community? Is it appropriate for a church to stage a demonstration against pornography? What about abuse of power in government? Can we be the "salt of the earth" if we are ineffective in retarding moral decay?

Something Worth Suffering For! (1:8-12)

Since God gives a spirit of power rather than timidity it follows that His servants have no excuse for failing to speak up for their Lord. Granted that in a first-century culture where the idea of a crucified Saviour was blasphemous to the Jews and sheer nonsense to the Gentiles (see 1 Cor. 1:23), it was not the easiest thing to do. It never is, even today. Yet God supplies the strength; all we do is to respond in obedience. Early in his letter to the church at Rome Paul wrote that he was not "ashamed of the gospel" because it was an instrument of God's power to bring

106

salvation to all who believe. It never let him down or put him to shame. Therefore he can declare with confidence to Timothy that there is no reason for reluctance or embarrassment in bearing witness to Christ.

Timothy is not to be ashamed of Paul either (see 2 Tim. 1:8). Although the apostle was put in chains by secular authorities he is, in the final analysis, a prisoner of Christ (note, "his [i.e., our Lord's] prisoner"). As George Matheson, the blind poet of Edinburgh, wrote:

> "Make me a captive, Lord,
>   and then I shall be free;
> Force me to render up my sword
>   and I shall conqueror be."

Rather than avoiding Paul the criminal, Timothy is to join with him in "suffering for the gospel." Later Paul will write that "everyone who wants to live a godly life in Christ Jesus will be persecuted" (3:12). Paradoxically, it is those who bring the "good news" (the gospel) who suffer. The world always has and always will be hostile to the only message that can heal its wounds (see John 15:18-25). Note that suffering for the gospel is carried out "in the strength that comes from God" (2 Tim. 1:8, *NEB*). He never asks us to do anything for which He will not supply the strength that we may carry it through. He *enables* us (causes us to be able) to bear the hardships that accompany the proclamation of the good news.

Some writers feel that verses 9 and 10 are taken from an early Christian hymn. Whether or not that is the case is of no great importance for our understanding. The unit is rich in theological truth. God saves and calls His own to a holy life. The plan was laid in the councils of eternity past. It was revealed through

107

the incarnation of Christ. Death is now destroyed and immortality has appeared.

God is the one who has saved us and called us to a life of holiness. It is important to understand that salvation is not simply deliverance from the penalty for sin. It is also the freedom to enter into a totally different kind of life. We are called to be holy. Peter exhorts, "Just as he who called you is holy, so be holy in all you do" (1 Pet. 1:15). There are no children of God who do not to some extent bear a family resemblance to their heavenly Father.

The New Testament doctrine of salvation by faith alone is summarized by the words, "Not because of anything we have done but because of his own purpose and grace" (2 Tim. 1:9; see Rom. 3:20-24; Phil. 3:8,9). God's saving action in history stems from His own purpose for mankind and is an expression of uncoerced and unmerited goodwill. This grace was given to us "in Christ Jesus," that is, by virtue of our faith in Christ. While God's goodwill may not be earned, it nevertheless must be received. Faith is not a human act that merits divine favor. It is man in his helplessness agreeing to let God do for him what he could never do for himself.

God's purpose to act in grace towards those who believe existed from "before the beginning of time." However only now has it been fully revealed. God has made plain His eternal plan for the redemption of man by sending His Son. Before the incarnation, death and resurrection of Christ it was not exactly clear how God would restore order in a moral universe made chaotic by the sinful rebellion of man. But now that our Saviour, Christ Jesus, has appeared (the latter word has a rich history in reference to the manifestation or enthronement of earthly dignitaries), death has been destroyed and life and immortality have been brought to light (see 1:10).

That Christ is designated *Saviour* takes on special meaning in that period of world history. Roman citizens at that time were being called upon to regard the emperor as divine. *"Kaisar Sōtēr"* (Caesar is Saviour) they were instructed to confess. But there is only one Saviour, and He is Jesus of Nazareth, God's Messiah (or Christ).

The work of Christ is described as twofold:

First, *He has "destroyed death."* First Corinthians 15:26 speaks of death as the "last enemy to be destroyed." And in Revelation 20:14 death is thrown into the lake of fire. So although it lingers in the present age as a necessary part of our physical finiteness, its power has once and for all been broken. It has lost its sting (see 1 Cor. 15:55) and no longer holds the believer in the captivity of fear (see Heb. 2:14,15).

Second, by means of the gospel, *life and immortality have been brought to light.* Before Christ the real meaning of eternal life was not clearly understood. But His triumphal resurrection and our present fellowship with the risen Lord illuminate what it means to possess by faith the real life which is immortality. "I have come," said Jesus, "that they may have life, and have it to the full" (John 10:10).

Paul can never forget his divine commission. Mention of the gospel moves him to affirm once again (see 1 Tim. 2:7) that it was to the proclamation of this message that he himself (the pronoun is emphatic) was appointed (2 Tim. 1:11). As herald he announced the good news of God's provision in Christ for the sins of man. As apostle he possessed the authority of a heavenly emissary. As teacher he explained the theological and ethical implications of the message.

The contemporary church needs to remember that

it exists as an ambassador of Christ (see 2 Cor. 5:20, 21). The message it bears to secular America and the world is that through Jesus Christ, God is reconciling the world to Himself. Thus we are to implore men to be reconciled to God (see 2 Cor. 5:18-20.) Ambassadors who fail to carry out their trust are guilty of gross negligence and even treason.

It is precisely because of the gospel that Paul is now suffering in prison. Yet he is not ashamed to be considered a common criminal. The reason for his confidence lies in a personal relationship he sustains with God his Father. He says, "I know whom I have believed" (2 Tim. 1:12). His faith is in a person, not a creed. Again we are reminded that the heart of the Christian faith is a personal relationship, not adherence to a doctrine or set of rules. While it is important to understand all we can about God from His revelation in Scripture, our confidence in the final analysis rests upon knowing him. "Beyond the sacred page," writes the hymnist, Mary A. Lathaway, "I seek *thee*, Lord. My spirit pants for *thee*, O Living Word" ("Break Thou the Bread of Life").

Since Paul *knows* on a personal basis the One in whom he has placed his trust, he is therefore thoroughly persuaded that God will guard what has been entrusted to Him. The Greek says simply "my deposit." It can mean "what I have placed in His safekeeping" or "what He has entrusted to me." The word is *parathēkē*, a legal term for that which has been turned over to a guardian for safekeeping. In both 1 Timothy 6:20 and 2 Timothy 1:14 it is that which is given by God to man. This would therefore appear to be its meaning in verse 12 as well. The point is that God will guard the faith He has entrusted to His spokesmen so that in the day of judgment they will be able to deliver it back to Him intact.

Apparently there has been from the beginning a natural reluctance about testifying for Christ. Paul needs to exhort Timothy not to be ashamed of speaking a word for the Lord. Rather he is to join with the apostle in suffering for the gospel. Context indicates that an open declaration of one's faith involves suffering. It appears that even the pastor of a church (Timothy in this case) can be ashamed of his faith in Christ.

Why do you suppose this is the case? Why is there a natural reluctance to share Christ with others? Do you eagerly anticipate every opportunity to speak out for the Lord? Is this reluctance tied up with the fact that we are still fallen human beings? Is the suffering that goes with testifying the suffering of anticipation or the suffering that follows as a result of obedience? Where does our reluctance ultimately stem from? How can this reluctance be overcome?

Keep the Faith (1:13,14)

The promise of divine help does not lessen the apostle's responsibility to guard the faith. Paul urges Timothy to "take as your model the sound teaching you have heard from me" (Kelly). Once again the Greek text helps us to see more vividly what Paul is saying. The word for pattern or model is *hupotupōsis*. It is used of the rough sketch an artist or architect might draw up or the outline a writer might develop prior to a fuller exposition. Paul's sound (or whole-some, health-giving) words are a *hupotupōsis*, a pattern for Timothy's ministry. He is not locked into teaching *only* what Paul has said. Rather, Paul's teaching provides the guidelines for Timothy's subsequent ministry.

Further, he is to maintain his orthodoxy in a spirit of "faith and love." These Christian virtues, so essential in all the activity of the church, are the result of

111

abiding "in Christ." *Goodspeed* has, "the faith and love that come through union with Christ Jesus." What God requires He also supplies. The Christian life was never intended to be lived by human effort alone. It is a supernatural life requiring a supernatural source of power.

This same truth is emphasized in verse 14. Timothy is to guard the noble deposit of truth. Yet his ability to carry out the responsibility comes from "the Holy Spirit who lives in us." Timothy is to keep the gospel free from error by reliance upon the indwelling Spirit. This is not a recommendation for uninformed reliance upon feeling. It is a call for appropriate reliance upon the Spirit of truth who Jesus promised would guide His followers "into all truth" (John 16: 13).

Paul viewed apostolic teaching as "sound"—that is, wholesome or healthy. The same word is used in Luke 5:31 where Jesus said that "it is not the *healthy* who need a doctor, but the sick" (italics added; see also 3 John 2). As good food produces good health, so does good religious instruction produce healthy Christians.

When the analogy is extended several questions arise. Can spiritual health exist apart from sound teaching? What is probably a major cause of sickness (spiritual) in Christians? Is spiritual sickness contagious? What sort of a menu would you suggest for a believer whose ill health shows up as anger and bitterness? What would you prescribe for spiritual flu? Can sick Christians recover without the health-giving properties of sound teaching?

A Friend in Need (1:15-18)

Paul has just charged Timothy with the responsibility of guarding the faith against error. Now he turns by way of example to those who deserted him (v. 15)

112

and to the one who continued faithful even to death (vv. 16-18). The implications would be clear to Timothy!

Since Paul spent some three years at Ephesus during his third missionary journey (see Acts 20:31) one would think that his converts there would be especially faithful. Unfortunately, now that he is once again in prison at Rome (a second imprisonment in the capital city separated from the account in Acts 28 by a journey to the western part of the empire), "everyone in the province of Asia" had abandoned him. The Roman province of Asia (not the continent) consisted of the western part of what is now Turkey plus the offshore islands. Its capital was Ephesus.

Among the deserters were two men, Phygelus and Hermogenes. We know nothing about them except that they abandoned Paul in his time of need. They may have been ringleaders in a major defection. Or— and I think this more probable—they may be mentioned because they were the kind of men who would be the least expected to defect. It is as if Paul is saying, "Even these two faithful brethren have deserted me in my hour of need."

Onesiphorus, however, is a different story. This Christian brother when in Rome searched Paul out and was unashamed of his chains. He visited him in prison not once but repeatedly. He "*often* refreshed me," says Paul (2 Tim. 1:16, italics added).

In a second-century writing, *The Acts of Paul and Thecla*, we learn that Onesiphorus was converted to the Christian faith while still a resident of Iconium, a city in which Paul ministered during his first missionary journey (see Acts 14:1-20). As a long-time friend (at least 15 years) Onesiphorus (whose name means "profitable"), unlike the Asian deserters, threw caution to the wind and searched diligently

113

throughout Rome until he found Paul (see 2 Tim. 1:17). Since Acts 28:30,31 presents Paul as staying in his own house in Rome, preaching and teaching to all who visited him, the desolate picture in 2 Timothy argues a second and later imprisonment. (On the basis of the Acts 28 passage Onesiphorus would have had no trouble in locating the apostle during his first imprisonment in Rome.)

We may assume that Paul had been portrayed to the Roman authorities as politically dangerous. To associate with him could result in sharing his fate. This did not deter the faithful Onesiphorus. His visits were "like a breath of fresh air" (2 Tim. 1:16, *TLB*). Paul's greatest needs at this point were not physical but personal and spiritual. He needed someone to stand by him in his hour of need. Onesiphorus was the man.

It is often discussed whether Onesiphorus had died by the time of Paul's letter. Perhaps so because Paul prays, "May the Lord grant that he will find mercy from the Lord on that day!" (v. 19). In 4:19 Paul sends greetings to the "household of Onesiphorus." It is on this basis that some claim to have in this passage precedent for praying for the dead. However verse 18 doesn't require that Onesiphorus be dead. It may only be a heartfelt expression that at the day of judgment the kindness of this friend be rewarded with mercy from God. It provides no solid base for the practice of prayers for the dead. Scripture elsewhere teaches that judgment follows death with no intervening period in which the activity of others can alter one's fate (see Luke 16:19-31).

Note the play on words: "he *found* me," may he then "*find* mercy from the Lord" (italics added). "That day" is the day of judgment. Note also that as a result of the faithfulness of Onesiphorus mercy is requested for his household (v. 16). No man lives to himself alone. Virtue reaps rich benefits for others as well. Finally Paul reminds them that they knew "better than [he] can tell [them]" *(NEB)* how many ways Onesiphorus had been of service in Ephesus.

Phygelus and Hermogenes, along with everyone else in Asia, had deserted Paul in his hour of need. They did not take a stand on behalf of the apostle. Onesiphorus, however, came to Rome and searched Paul out. He was unashamed of the apostle's chains. His loyalty and personal devotion were a great boon to the apostle in his time of need. Paul says of Onesiphorus that "he often refreshed me."

Can you think of any modern situation that parallels the relationship of Paul and Onesiphorus? Who today is suffering for the faith? Who today needs the refreshment of a friend who will stand by and associate himself with the one in need? Beyond that, do we bring refreshment to one another? Can you think of certain Christians who always leave you refreshed? Are there some who leave you feeling worse? How do you affect others? When you leave are they better off (or worse off) than they were when you showed up? To what extent are we obliged to refresh one another?

8

SECOND TIMOTHY TWO

Pass It On (2:1,2)

Chapter divisions in Scripture are normally helpful, but occasionally they disrupt a sequence of thought that should remain intact. We encounter such an interruption here. In the previous chapter Timothy was reminded of his ordination, of Paul's total commitment to the gospel and of the stirring example of Onesiphorus' faithfulness. Now Paul continues, "You" (the pronoun is emphatic) "then, my son, be strong. At your ordination you pledged yourself to the ministry. I have remained faithful even though it has led to imprisonment. Onesiphorus has kept the faith. Now, Timothy, you too be strong in the grace which is ours by virtue of our union with Christ Jesus."

Specifically Timothy is to transmit to reliable men what he has learned from Paul. The reference is not so much to teaching in general which Timothy may have heard from Paul but to the apostolic gospel itself —to the "deposit" which was entrusted to him (1:14). Timothy heard these things from Paul "in the presence of many witnesses" (2:2). Apparently Paul had some specific occasion in mind when the gospel message had been formally transmitted to Timothy. Perhaps at his ordination a summary of apostolic truth was recited as part of the official ceremony. Many witnesses were present who would attest the ordination and all it involved.

Timothy is now to entrust the same message to other men. They must meet two requirements:

They must be reliable. Elsewhere Paul has written that "it is required that those who have been given a trust must prove faithful" (1 Cor. 4:2). In the parable of the talents the two servants who used their resources wisely were each commended by the master, "Well done, good and faithful servant!" (Matt. 25:21,23). No virtue is quite so necessary in the life of the church as reliability.

They must be capable of teaching others. This does not require skills available only to those who have formal training in educational methods. An understanding of the truth and a personal desire to share it with others is all that is necessary.

Verse 2 sets the pattern for the transmission of apostolic teaching. It is men training men. Multiplication is God's method. While in the early days before the New Testament had been completed this process was especially crucial to guarantee that the gospel would remain free from error, the process itself still has validity for contemporary evangelism and Christian growth.

Faithfulness is a crucial factor in the efficient operation of any social organization. Unless each member of the group carries out his assigned role the entire movement will gradually grind to a halt. The church needs faithful men. Timothy is to entrust the apostolic message to *reli-*

able men—men who are competent and can be trusted to transmit the gospel to others.

In the local congregation, to whom are believers to be faithful? Can a person be faithful to God without being faithful at the same time to God's people? Does faithfulness in a church setting mean that one must always agree with the decision of the leadership? Should the Christian not be reliable if he believes that he has a better way to achieve the desired goal? Can such minor irritations as habitual tardiness and lack of financial support be labeled lack of reliability? Can you be counted on?

Soldiers, Athletes and Farmhands (2:3-7)

Paul had a way of getting his point across by using illustrations from daily life which everyone would understand. The soldier's concentration of energies, the athlete's self-discipline, and the farmhand's hard work are all characteristics absolutely necessary for the Christian ministry. At the close of the paragraph (see v. 7) Paul tells Timothy, "Reflect on what I am saying," or, as *Phillips* has it, "Consider these three illustrations of mine." As Timothy reflects on what Paul has been saying he may count on the Lord to give him the insight necessary to grasp the full implications of the teaching.

Timothy is called upon to "endure hardship" like a professional soldier (v. 3). The task of ministry was never intended to be trouble-free. It involves hardship. In another place Paul indicates what his apostleship costs him—hard work, prison, flogging, exposure to death, stoning, shipwreck, every conceivable sort of danger, sleepless nights, hunger and thirst, cold and exposure, and beyond all this, the daily pressure of concern for the churches (see 2 Cor. 11:23-28). Being a soldier in the army of God is not child's play. It is no place for the uncommitted.

118

Two characteristics of a good soldier are mentioned:

First, *he does not get "involved in civilian affairs"* (2 Tim. 1:4). A soldier on active duty cannot get entangled with the affairs of everyday life. He must renounce every involvement that would hinder him from carrying out his primary role as a fighting man. Barclay notes that the Roman code of Theodosius said, "We forbid men engaged on military service to engage in civilian occupations." The Christian soldier likewise must remain detached from the secular concerns of this world. Although living in the world he remains combat ready. While there is nothing intrinsically wrong with "civilian pursuits" *(RSV)*, they become wrong the moment they entangle the Christian so as to diminish his usefulness in the army of God.

Second, *a good soldier "wants to please his commanding officer."* "He must be wholly at his commanding officer's disposal" *(NEB)*. In the heat of battle there is no place for a soldier who, on the basis of his limited view of the conflict, resists the orders of his superior officer who understands the total war plan. It is obedience that "pleases" a commanding officer.

To illustrate further the Christian ministry Paul turns to athletic games. If an athlete desires the victor's crown he must compete "according to the rules" (v. 5). Although cheating seems to be the point in question it doesn't fit the demands of the larger context. It is obvious that a runner can't cut corners on the track or a discus thrower use a lightweight discus.

A clue for interpretation is found in the word "lawfully" (v. 5, *KJV*). The official regulations for the Olympic games included rules about the training period. According to Pausanias, a second-century

Greek historian, competitors in the Olympic games had to swear that they had been in strict training for 10 months before the contest. The purpose was to maintain high standards and to insure that the competitors were only those who had submitted themselves to severe self-discipline.

Ministry requires self-discipline. It is no place for those unwilling to pay the price of personal commitment. In order to run the race we are to "throw off everything that hinders" (Heb. 12:1). Activities and pursuits not necessarily wrong in themselves become wrong for those who are in divine training (see 1 Tim. 4:7).

Paul draws his third illustration from farming. He reasons that the laborer who is actually doing the work has a prior claim to share in the crop. Those who dawdle or don't work at all do not qualify. Here the emphasis is on the hard work or toil of the ministry. God's great field is not harvested by lazy preachers or laymen. Some writers feel that Paul is reminding Timothy of his right to share in the material welfare of his parishioners. It is better, however, to take it as an exhortation to hard work. In this way it remains parallel with the two previous illustrations.

The idea of a soldier leaving the front lines every afternoon so as to be able to return to his grocery store or law office and keep things running is ludicrous. Soldiers have a supreme commitment to the defense and welfare of their country. They are not allowed to get entangled in civilian pursuits. A commanding officer would never put up with divided loyalties of that sort. The church requires good soldiers who will endure hardships and steer clear of civilian entanglements.

List some civilian pursuits which have no place in the life of a Christian. Are any of these good in themselves? What is it about the Christian faith that makes wrong something which would be permissible on secular grounds? Do you think the cause of Christ would be benefited if all believers reorganized their priorities so as to reduce the number of nonessential "civilian affairs"? Do you think this will ever happen apart from individual believers (you and I) taking the step? Why do we hesitate?

Chained Like a Criminal (2:8-13)

Paul has made his appeal to Timothy on several bases: his ordination vows; his godly parentage; the example of the apostle's life; the faithfulness of Onesiphorus; the logic of illustrations drawn from daily life. Now he sets forth the most powerful argument of all—"Keep before your mind Jesus Christ" (v. 8, *TCNT*). The point is that even Christ Himself had to pass through suffering before He was exalted. He "learned obedience from what he suffered" (Heb. 5:8). It was because He became "obedient to death—even death on a cross!" that God "exalted him to the highest place" (Phil. 2:8,9). And Peter adds that Christ left us an example of suffering so that we should follow in His steps (see 1 Pet. 2:21). The early church was convinced that to live for Christ one must be prepared for hardship and suffering. Timothy needed to adjust himself to this stern reality.

Most writers think that verse 8 contains a fragment of an early Christian creed. Jesus Christ is presented as (1) risen from the dead, and (2) descended from David. These two phrases treat the two natures of Christ. That He was fully man follows from His earthly lineage. That He is fully God is attested by His resurrection. Romans 1 indicates that He was declared Son of God "by his resurrection from the dead" (v. 4; note both His Davidic lineage and His resurrection in verses 3,4). The tense of the verb stresses not only the fact of the Resurrection but the resulting condition. Christ is forever risen and present in His resurrection power.

"This," says Paul, "is [the heart of] my gospel"— the essence of what I preach (2 Tim. 2:8). And it is because I preach this message that I am now suffering "even to the extent of wearing chains as though I were a criminal" (v. 9, *Williams*). The word for "criminal" was used of those who were guilty of gross misdeeds and serious crimes. Elsewhere in the New Testament it is found only in Luke 23:32,39 where it is used of the two criminals who were crucified along with Jesus.

While Paul knows that the real reason for his imprisonment is his preaching of the gospel it is probable that the charges leveled against him were political. The Roman empire at that time covered most of the known world. It included many conquered groups. Hence the Roman officials were extremely wary about any kind of association that could disrupt the peace and welfare of the empire. As the leader of a religious sect that would not honor the emperor by offering a sacrifice to him, Paul was constantly in danger of being taken for a rabble-rouser and traitor. His actual imprisonment appears to have been the result of Nero's decision to blame Christians for his own folly in setting fire to Rome.

Paul knew that even though he was in chains the Word of God was not. The preacher may be imprisoned but the message cannot be bound. At another time and from another jail Paul wrote to the church at Philippi telling them that what had happened to him had actually served to advance the gospel. The palace guard had been evangelized and Christians had become increasingly bold in witnessing (see Phil. 1:13,14).

Paul is willing to go through all kinds of hardship, even being treated like a common criminal, so that the elect may gain salvation in Christ Jesus. It would appear that the elect of verse 10 are those chosen by God who do not as yet believe. If this is the case then Paul sees his suffering as part of the total price required to bring the elect to salvation. Some interpret the verse in the light of Colossians 1:24 to mean that a predetermined amount of suffering on the part of the church is necessary before the end can come. It may be, however, that salvation here is to be thought of as that complete deliverance from sin which begins at the moment of faith (justification), continues through life (sanctification), and is completed when we are ushered into the presence of God (glorification). The final phrase, "with eternal glory," would support this interpretation. The sufferings of Paul, then, would be on behalf of all believers, not simply those who will someday come to faith.

We now come to the fourth "trustworthy saying" in the letters to Timothy (see 1 Tim. 1:15; 3:1; 4:9). It is undoubtedly taken from an early Christian hymn. Its purpose is to show the close connection between suffering and glory for those who share in the fellowship of Christ.

The first strophe (or short stanza) asserts that it is those who have died with Him who will also live with Him. The reference is to baptism. The entire sixth chapter of Romans is built on the theological foundation of the Christian's death to sin and his resurrection to new life as symbolized by baptism (see esp. vv. 3,4). To live one must first die—this is the great paradox of faith. Jesus taught that to save life one must lose it (Luke 9:24).

The hymn in 2 Timothy chapter 2 continues by noting that it is those who endure who will also reign with Christ. This reference to suffering or patient endurance probably explains the inclusion of the hymn at this point in Paul's letter. It is as if Paul is saying, "Endure hardship," Timothy (v. 3) because that is what Jesus went through (v. 8) and, as we often sing, "If we endure, we will also reign with him" (v. 12). (Reference to the reign of believers is found in Revelation 5:10 as well.)

Then follows the other possibility, "If we disown him, he will also disown us." This is exactly what Jesus taught in Matthew 10:33. Disowning or refusing to acknowledge Christ in this life will inevitably result in His disowning us at the final judgment. It is a serious matter to draw back from allegiance to Christ.

The final strophe (v. 13) presents a slight problem. When taken as parallel with the previous stanzas we might expect it to read, "If we are faithless, He will be disloyal to us." Instead we learn that our faithlessness is countered by His loyalty. This must never be taken as an escape clause for apostasy. It does not teach that believers may give up their faith in Christ and count on Him to hold them guiltless at the last judgment. This would be contrary to New Testament teaching in general, to say nothing of the warning in the immediately preceding verse ("If we disown him, he will also disown us"). It is intended for those believers with overly sensitive consciences who feel they may somehow have failed to accomplish perfectly all that could be expected of them.

We may depend upon God to acknowledge the faithful and also to disown those who fall away. The reason is evident, "He cannot be untrue to himself" *(Goodspeed)*. Or, as one writer puts it, "The moral impossibility of self-contradiction in God forms the basis of His faithfulness" (Guthrie).

Paul declares that the gospel for which he was suffering consisted of (1) the resurrection of Jesus Christ from the dead, and (2) the Davidic descent of Jesus. In other words the gospel is that Jesus of Nazareth was fully man (He came in the human line of David) and also fully God (He rose from the dead).

Why do unbelievers object to this gospel? Apart from the bodily resurrection of Jesus what could we know for sure about life beyond the grave? In what way does the resurrection of Christ demonstrate that His teaching is true?

Of what help is it to us that Jesus is fully man? To what extent does the Davidic descent of Jesus validate prophecy? Explain the uniqueness of Jesus Christ.

Correctly Handling the Word of Truth (2:14-19)

Once again Paul's deep concern about the false teachers at Ephesus surfaces (see 1 Tim. 1:3-7, 19,20; 4:1-8; 6:3-5,20,21). Timothy is to keep on reminding the congregation of the essentials of the Christian faith. He is to warn them against getting caught up in petty quarrels over words. It is useless to argue nonessentials and serves only to demoralize everyone who listens.

Language is a remarkable gift. It is intended to promote communication and understanding. But like all God's gifts it can be twisted to serve other ends. While the Christian faith has a rational content capable of being expressed in words, it is not the sum total of those words. In essence it is an act of faith in the redemptive act of God. It is a path to walk, not a philosophy to discuss. The false teachers at Ephesus were turning the adventure of faith into a philosophical debate. Both they and all who listened came out losers. The verb "ruins," *katastrophē* (compare our English "catastrophe"), means literally "turning upside down." It is the opposite of edification (building up) which is so central a concern in Paul's writings (see 1 Cor. 14:26; Eph. 4:12; etc.). Vain argumentation turns people upside down—it does not build them up.

Instead of quarreling about words Timothy is to do his very best to present himself to God as a workman who has been tested and approved as both competent and faithful (see 2 Tim. 2:15). While the troublemakers sought to gain the favor of men, Timothy's approval was to come from God.

Shoddy workmanship is the public confession of a careless attitude. Timothy is to pursue his task with all diligence so that he will never have to be ashamed of what he has done. There will be no cause for shame if he "correctly handles the word of truth." This phrase, rendered by the King James translators as "rightly dividing the word of truth," has been the subject of much discussion. The problem (if there is one) stems from the Greek word *orthotomeō* which occurs only here in the New Testament (it is also found twice in the Greek version of the Old Testament: Prov. 3:6 and 11:5). Literally it means "to cut straight." Elsewhere in Greek literature it is used in such contexts as a farmer plowing a straight furrow or a mason cutting a stone to a correct pattern. In our present context it means handling the word of truth in a straightforward manner, that is, without deviating into the crooked paths of the false teachers. It does not refer to dividing Scripture into time periods or dispensations for the purpose of correct interpretation.

Timothy is to avoid worldly and empty chatter. Those who indulge in it become more and more ungodly. There is a bit of irony in Paul's choice of words. In verse 16 "will become" translates the

126

Greek *prokoptō*, to advance or progress. Literally it means "to cut down in front," that is, to remove obstacles and move ahead. It appears that the false teachers were claiming progress on the basis of cutting down a number of Christian doctrines (a bodily resurrection for one; see 2 Tim. 2:18) which slowed down their advance. They *are* making progress, says Paul, but it is "progress" in the wrong direction! They are progressing further and further into godlessness.

Unless the activities of the false teachers are stopped their teaching will continue to spread like gangrene, infecting the entire Body of Christ at Ephesus (see v. 17). The problem of error would not be as serious if it affected only those who taught it. Unfortunately this is not the case. Others, intrigued by the lure of deceptive doctrine, are drawn into the movement.

Hymenaeus and Philetus are singled out for special mention. In his earlier letter Paul speaks of Hymenaeus as one of two men whom he excommunicated (see 1 Tim. 1:20). That he was still around shows the seriousness of the problem at Ephesus. Philetus is nowhere else mentioned.

These two men strayed from the path of truth by teaching that the Resurrection had already taken place (see 2 Tim. 2:18). While ancient peoples generally believed in some sort of immortality, they would not readily accept the idea of a physical resurrection. The Greeks thought of the soul as an immortal entity imprisoned in a physical body. Death released the soul from its earthly prison, allowing it to be reabsorbed into God. Even within Judaism the powerful sect of the Sadducees denied the Resurrection (see Acts 23:8).

Against this background it is easy to see why some who were more interested in currying favor with men than in remaining faithful to God would try to explain away the doctrine of the Resurrection. Hymenaeus and Philetus said it had "already taken place." That is, they taught that in his union with Christ the believer had already undergone a spiritual resurrection and that this resurrection was all there would ever be. Error always contains some element of truth. The truth is that in a spiritual sense the believer *has* "been raised with Christ" (Col. 3:1). The error is in stopping at this point and denying that there will be a physical resurrection in the future. This subtle twisting of the truth was playing havoc with the faith of some within the church. No wonder Paul was concerned.

In spite of the heretical teaching which had infiltrated the church Paul is able to remind Timothy that the firm foundation laid by God continues to stand (2 Tim. 2:19). Jesus established the church upon the solid foundation of Peter's great confession that Jesus was the Christ, the Son of the living God. Nothing, not even the forces of the underworld, would be able to overpower the church (see Matt. 16:16,18).

Paul often used the metaphor of a building to illustrate some aspect of the church (1 Cor. 3:10-15; Eph. 2:19-22). Here, in 2 Timothy 2:19-21, he alludes to the practice of engraving inscriptions on buildings in order to designate ownership or purpose. The church bears two inscriptions:

The first is, *"The Lord knows those who are his."* Timothy should remember that in spite of the confusion caused by error at Ephesus, God knows who are really His own. He can distinguish true believers from those who are turning away from the truth.

The second inscription is, *"Everyone who confesses the name of the Lord must turn away from wickedness."* It follows logically that Christians may be de-

128

fined as those who forsake evil. There is no biblical teaching to support the idea that after one is saved it doesn't matter how he lives. In Romans 8:14 Paul limits the sons of God to those who are *being led* by the Spirit of God. (The previous verse teaches that those who "live according to the sinful nature . . . will die.") In the words of the title of a famous book by William Law, this is *A Serious Call to a Devout and Holy Life.*

Paul is deeply concerned about the false teachers at Ephesus. He has referred to them on several occasions. They appear to have been an argumentative lot who took a rather perverse delight in using words to trip up believers. Timothy is to warn them against "waging word-battles" (2 Tim. 2:14, *Rhm*). Other translations call it "wrangling about words" or "petty debating."

From time to time in Sunday School or home Bible studies, discussions turn into minor disputes about peripheral matters. How is it possible to stay away from such debates? Is it spiritually edifying to win a religious argument? How about losing a religious argument? What is the intended outcome of Bible study? Is the Christian faith primarily a walk or a doctrine? Is it possible on occasion that the drive to understand more clearly is really an attempt to substitute theory for practice? Do you find this a temptation?

Don't Argue with the Opposition (2:20-26)

Some writers consider verses 20,21 as a conclusion to the preceding paragraph. Timothy is to separate himself from men like Hymenaeus and Philetus in order to be able to carry out the work of the Lord. Others take the verses as preparing the way for the personal exhortations which follow. We understand them to be an integral part of Paul's continuing discussion, related both to the false teachers just mentioned and the exhortation he is about to give. For convenience we bracket the verses with what follows.

The church is like a large house in which there are dishes and utensils not only of gold and silver but also of wood and clay. Some are for noble purposes while others serve menial ends. By the illustration Paul means that in the church there are various kinds of people. Some are for honorable uses and others for dishonorable. (The same two words are used of pots made by the potter; see Rom. 9:21.) Undoubtedly there is a backward glance toward the two false teachers of 2 Timothy 4:17.

Paul handles the figure fairly loosely as he continues. If a man cleanses himself from whatever is dishonorable he will be "an instrument for noble purposes" (v. 21). While it is God alone who has cleansed us by the washing for regeneration (see Titus 3:5) it is up to us to cleanse ourselves from the daily contact with sin (see John 13:10). Three things are said of the one who by cleansing himself is a noble vessel. (1) He has been set apart for a holy purpose. That is what it means to be "sanctified" or "made holy." (2) He is "useful to the Master." What greater honor exists than to serve the King of kings! (3) He is "prepared to do any good work." The reward for holiness is not some special honor but the opportunity for additional service.

It should be mentioned that a number of writers have taken verse 21 to mean that Timothy is to separate himself from the heretical teachers. This would enable him to carry out his prescribed role. This appears less likely. Timothy is elsewhere told to take positive action in relation to the heretics (see 1 Tim. 1:3), not to withdraw from them.

Timothy is counseled to run away ("flee") from the

130

cravings of youth and run toward ("pursue") the virtues of Christian maturity (2 Tim. 2:22). "Evil desires," as the *New International Version* puts it, is too strong a translation for the Greek *epithumia* which may be used in a neutral or even a good sense. (In Phil. 1:23 it is used of Paul's desire to be with Christ.) The desires or cravings of youth are those attitudes and actions that contrast with Christian maturity (e.g., desire to argue, quick temper, lack of patience, etc.). Continue to grow up, Timothy my son, is what Paul is saying. Strive for "righteousness, faith, love and peace" (2 Tim. 2:22; 1 Tim. 6:11 treats the first three). This is best carried out in association with "those who call on the Lord out of a pure heart." Fellowship with other sincere believers is the proper setting for Christian growth. The church is a body and the development of each member is aided significantly by the health of the entire organism. Paul's statement, "None of us lives to himself alone" (Rom. 14:7), while given in another context, is equally applicable here.

Verse 23 is yet another warning to stay away from foolish and ill-informed speculation. All they do is to produce quarrels and the Lord's servant has no business quarreling. While this is generally true of all believers it is especially true of church leaders.

Instead of quarreling Timothy is to display four positive virtues (v. 24): First, Timothy is to *be "courteous to every one"* (*TCNT*). This translation reflects the intended contrast with "must not quarrel." God's work cannot be carried on in an atmosphere charged with anger and resentment. The Christian must be a gentle person.

Second, Timothy is to *"be a skillful teacher" (Williams).* The emphasis is not on the amount of knowledge he has but on his ability to put across his point.

Third, he must *be "ready to overlook grievances"* *(Norlie)*. There is no place for resentment in the life of a Christian leader. It eats away at the one who imagines he has been wronged and spreads a grim pessimism that affects everyone else.

Fourth, he must *instruct his opponents with gentleness* (v. 25). The choice of words suggests that those who hold differing opinions do so because of lack of appropriate information. This is certainly putting the best interpretation on the acts and attitudes of the opposition. It is a display of the kindness Paul is calling for. As a result it is hoped that God will give them a change of heart which will lead to the knowledge of the truth. Note that repentance is a gift of God. He is the one who changes men's hearts. Without His divine intervention no one could turn himself about and seek the truth. By nature there is "not one who is searching for God!" (Rom. 3:11, *TCNT*).

In 2 Timothy 2:26 Paul expresses the hope that the opponents will sober up and escape the devil's trap. "Come to their senses" means to return to sobriety. The false teachers are pictured as intoxicated and therefore unable to think straight. They are also entrapped by the devil to do his will. They need to escape. Elsewhere Paul talks about believers as having been "slaves to sin" but now being "slaves to God" (Rom. 6:20,22). Timothy's gentle instruction is intended to lead men to see the error of their way so that by repentance they may throw off their slavery to error and sin. It is a calling worthy of Timothy's most rigorous self-discipline and full commitment to personal spiritual maturity.

Paul counsels Timothy to pursue Christian virtue "along with those who call on the Lord out of a pure heart" (2 Tim. 2:22). Some have interpreted the individualism of Protestantism to mean that believers can gain little from congregational association. The priesthood of every believer is held to imply that every man is on his own when it comes to spiritual growth. Paul would disagree. The Christian virtues are to be pursued in concert with other believers who share the same spiritual goals. The major metaphor of the church is the body. We grow individually only as we grow together.

What functions in the modern church help bind the members together as the Body of Christ? Which tend to separate? Should members of a local church share only in "spiritual" activities or is there a valid place for such things as picnics, fun nights, basketball, etc.? How important do you feel it is that young people in the church have much of their social life within the fellowship of the congregation? Does the contemporary breakdown of the family have its counterpart in a breakdown of fellowship within the community of believers or is the church compensating for the erosion of family ties?

9

SECOND TIMOTHY THREE

It's Bad and Getting Worse (3:1-9)

Jewish thought divided time into two distinct ages —the present age (troubled and sinful) and the age to come (blessed and ruled by God). The transition would involve a period of intense distress. Similarly the New Testament teaches a period of spiritual and social collapse to precede the return of Christ. This period is called "the last days." Paul writes, "The final age of this world is to be a time of troubles" *(NEB)*. Peter, as well, speaks of scoffing and evil desires that will characterize the "last days" (2 Pet. 3:3).

While the writers of the New Testament taught that this period of stress would come at the end of the age, it should be noted that they saw themselves as already having entered that period. The author of Hebrews writes of how God spoke in days gone past and then adds, "But in *these last days* he has spoken to us by his Son" (Heb. 1:2, italics added). From the New Testament standpoint the "age to come" (the messianic era) began with the resurrection of Christ and the coming of the Holy Spirit. Its complete manifestation awaits the return of Christ. The spiritual and social collapse which marks the end is already beginning to take place in Paul's day. Note that the verbs in verses 6-9 are in the present tense, not the future.

That which qualifies the last days as "terrible times" is the moral collapse of people. They are described in terms that offer no glimmer of hope. The vices are listed mostly in pairs. Paul seems to be drawing upon his rhetorical skill in preaching. He begins by listing the two things upon which man has set his affection. Man is a lover of himself and a lover of money. Self-centeredness is the fundamental and basic sin. Adam sinned because he wanted to advance himself rather than remain obedient to divinely imposed limitations. As a result Self reigns in the heart of every human being born into this world. By nature we are self-centered. Only by a supernatural deliverance made possible by the indwelling Holy Spirit can Self be dethroned and Christ given His rightful place as Lord of our lives.

Verses 2-4 begin by listing what men love. It closes in the same way. In the last days people will be "lovers of pleasure rather than lovers of God." Personal gratification is a consuming passion of man. In recent laboratories it has been shown that rats will endure almost anything in order to have their pleasure centers electrically stimulated. Insofar as natural man is governed by a compulsive concern for pleasure he lives on a level shared by the animal world. But redeemed humanity is controlled by love for God, not by the pursuit of pleasure. The list of vices is thus bracketed by a trinity of misplaced affections. Man loves himself, money and pleasure. These, however, can never give satisfaction because man was created to love God. He is haunted by an awareness of God.

The list itself needs little explanation. "Boastful"

refs to the outward behavior of a person who is inwardly "proud." "Abusive" ("blasphemers," *KJV*) and "disobedient to their parents" describe improper and unnatural conduct in relation to people in general and specifically toward one's own father and mother. In the last days people will be without gratitude and "refuse to recognize even the ultimate decencies of life" (Barclay).

The description of godless society in the last days continues. Men will be "without love," or, as the King James Version has it, "without natural affection" (the Greek usage suggests lack of normal family affection). The contemporary breakdown of the family unit is an expression of this prophetic declaration. The "unforgiving" are those who simply will not come to terms with others.

Human society in the last days is described as made up of people who are "slanderous [malicious gossips], without self-control [unable to curb evil desires], brutal [savage—the opposite of civilized], not lovers of the good [hostile to all that is worthy of respect], treacherous [perhaps a hint that some believers had become informers for the Roman empire], rash [one swept on by sudden impulse], conceited [swollen with self-importance]." This stark picture of man without God is terrifying in the extreme. It reminds the Christian of his strategic role as the "salt of the earth" (Matt. 5:13)—that which retards the moral deterioration of society.

Finally Paul writes that the last days will be marked by people who "maintain a facade of 'religion'" *(Phillips)* but "refuse to let it be a power" *(Beck)*. Religious observances continue but any idea of the gospel as a dynamic force is rejected. Such people conform to the ritual requirements of religion but hold that religion is nothing more than that.

136

Power upsets and transforms. People want a religion that requires nothing and changes nothing. A bit of rustic tradition totally inoffensive to anyone. Keep away from people like that, is Paul's advice to Timothy. This charge indicates that the terrible times of the last days were already present in the first century A.D.

Among these religious people who are convinced that the gospel has no real power (see v. 5), are those who have managed to work their way into homes and captivate weak-willed and silly women. Two things are said about the method of these disruptive reprobates. First, they "worm their way" into homes (v. 6). The Greek word has the idea of gaining access by the use of deceit. Second, they "gain control" or capture (the noun form is "prisoner") the women. Some have suggested a Gnostic background at this point. It will be remembered that Gnosticism taught the absolute distinction between spirit and matter. The evil nature of matter (contrasted with spirit as good) led logically to one of two conclusions about the body. Either it should be denied (asceticism) or allowed whatever it may desire (licentiousness). It is possible that the "weak-willed women" of the Ephesian church had either separated themselves from normal physical relationships with their husbands (option 1) or entered into promiscuous arrangements with the false teachers (option 2). In any case, they had fallen under the spell of theological charlatans with the result that the congregation was seriously affected.

It should be noted once again (see commentary on (1 Tim. 3:9) that in Paul's day women had been deprived of adequate education and social equality. As a result the average Greek woman lived a rather secluded life and would be easy prey for religious propagandists who could get her ear. Woman's place in the first-century church is spelled out in 1 Timothy 2:11-15.

Paul goes on to describe the "miserable women" *(NEB)* in four ways:

First, they are *"loaded down with sins."* The picture is one of a person laboring under a heavy load of guilt. Moffatt's translation describes them as those "who feel crushed by the burden of their sins." *Phillips* thinks they have "an exaggerated sense of sin" but that does not square with the description that follows. They *feel* guilty because they *are* guilty.

Second, they are *"swayed by all kinds of evil desires."* Unstable individuals. Vulnerable to every evil craving.

Third, they are always *wide-open to every new doctrine.* They have a perverse curiosity about every theological fad that comes along. One writer speaks of the dangers connected with "intellectual curiosity without moral earnestness." Undiscerning open-mindedness is no friend of truth.

Fourth, in spite of their avid pursuit of "knowledge" they are *unable to arrive at a personal understanding of truth* (see v. 7). Truth reveals itself only to those who are willing to act upon it. To disobey what one knows to be right is to cut oneself off from any further knowledge of God. We progress in understanding as we obey in conduct. The Ephesian women were doomed to the "quest for truth" because they had decided against truth itself. Captivated by the merchants of error they became prisoners to their own deceitful passions. No one is so blind as the one who will not see.

The false teachers at Ephesus "oppose the truth" in the same way as Jannes and Jambres "opposed Moses" (v. 8). These two names are supplied by non-biblical sources for Pharaoh's court magicians whose attempts to match the miracles of Moses were at first successful but later failed (see Exod. 7:11; 8:7; 9:11). In Jewish legend they came to typify anyone who would oppose the will of God and try to frustrate His purposes. The heretics at Ephesus, says Paul, are no more than a couple of evil sorcerers who would by deceit keep God's children in bondage. They are utterly corrupt in mind and "counterfeits so far as faith is concerned" *(MLB)*. In an earlier letter Paul wrote of similar men who "suppress the truth by their wickedness" and whose thinking "became futile" (Rom. 1:18,21).

Paul is certain that the false teachers will not be able to make any further progress (see v. 9; a better translation than the *NIV*'s "not get very far"—they had *already* gone too far!) because, like Jannes and Jambres, their foolishness will be evident to all. Impostors are inevitably disclosed for what they really are.

Human nature has not changed over the course of history. While culture has "advanced," man's basic characteristics remain the same. This is what makes Scripture ever relevant. The basic human problems of the first century are still the basic problems of the twentieth. Paul writes of those who are forever getting information but unable to come to a personal understanding of truth (v. 7). This is especially true of those who put aside the revelation of God in Scripture (if they in fact ever paid any attention to it) and sought wisdom and understanding from purely secular sources.

Is there any question that the believer has in Scripture the source of all wisdom? How much, if any, divine revelation is found outside the Bible? To what extent, if any, do secular answers to human problems fulfill man's need? Can psychology help? How much? Is what secular moralists say wrong? Can the believer salvage insights from secular sources or does *all* his wisdom come from God? How would you explain the difference between knowledge and personal understanding? How does the former become the latter?

Nurtured on Scripture (3:10-17)

In contrast to the false teachers, Timothy has "followed, step by step" (v. 10, *NEB*) the example of Paul's life and teaching. The verb in this context does not mean to "know all about" (*NIV*) in the sense of being fully informed. It means rather to "follow as an example."

It is important to note that the first thing Timothy has faithfully followed is the apostle's teaching. Doctrine is important. Apart from a theological basis there is no compelling reason why a person should adopt any particular ethical standard for living. On the other hand, if God is holy (theological doctrine) then His followers must also be holy (ethical implication). Remove God from the equation and man is free to do whatever he can get by with.

Paul's way of life was clearly known to Timothy. The two had been intimate associates in the early outreach of the church. Timothy had traveled with Paul as an apprentice from the time of the second missionary journey (about A.D. 51). He had watched the apostle in all sorts of situations. He knew firsthand of Paul's chief aim in life, his confidence in God, his patience, kindly concern, and steadfastness.

Timothy also knew of the many persecutions (see v. 11) Paul had endured—specifically at Antioch (where the leading citizens ran him out of town, Acts 13:50), Iconium (where he barely escaped a stoning, Acts 14:5) and Lystra (where he was stoned, dragged out of town, and left for dead, Acts 14:19). Yet Timo-

140

thy also knew that the Lord had rescued Paul from every assault upon his life. The apostle had not been spared suffering but he had never been forgotten by God or left to die at the hands of men. The theme of God as deliverer is found repeatedly in the Psalms. Psalm 34:17 says that "the righteous cry out, and the Lord hears them; he delivers them from all their troubles." God has always been available to rescue those who place their trust in Him.

A basic principle of the Christian life is that every person who has determined to live a devout and holy life in union with Christ Jesus will meet with persecution (see v. 12). Jesus told His disciples, "All men will hate you because of me" (Matt. 10:22). Shortly after Paul suffered abuse in the cities mentioned in verse 11 (Antioch, Iconium, Lystra) he returned to instruct the believers there, saying, "We must go through many hardships to enter the kingdom of God" (Acts 14:22). The men of this world will never embrace a religious system whose ethical requirements stand in judgment of the way they like to live. Sin will always oppose righteousness. Since the perfect man, Christ Jesus, was crucified for His sinless life and candid testimony concerning God His Father, there is little possibility that the world will gladly accept those who diligently pursue a life in conformity to Christ's. If believers today are not meeting persecution it is not because the world has come to appreciate goodness. It is rather because so few believers have determined to live genuinely Christian lives.

As time passes "evil men and impostors will go from bad to worse" (2 Tim. 3:13). The word translated "impostors" means literally "magicians." This is a direct reference to those in Ephesus who qualified as contemporary counterparts to Jannes and Jambres (see v. 7). Some see an allusion to the practice of

141

magic arts (see Acts 19:19 where believers at Ephesus publicly burned magic scrolls valued at over a million dollars in today's currency!).

The heretics are said to be "advancing" (Greek, "to cut forward") backwards (note the irony). Their conduct is taking them in the wrong direction. They are "deceiving and being deceived." Like Satan, "that ancient serpent . . . who leads the whole world astray" (Rev. 12:9), they make progress by deceiving others. Words become the tools of deception rather than the means for understanding. In the process of deceiving, the false teachers are themselves deceived. One of the penalties for misleading others is a vulnerability toward being misled. Sin is inevitably repaid in kind.

In marked contrast to the evil impostors whose major weapon is deceit, Timothy is to remain faithful to the truths he has learned and knows to be true (2 Tim. 3:14). The Christian faith is not a philosophy that must adjust to every cultural trend. It is a declaration of what God did once and for all in Jesus Christ for the salvation of man and what this implies about the conduct of those who by faith enter into a personal relationship with the risen Lord. It deals in absolutes and as such continues unchanged throughout time. The bodily resurrection of Christ is as much a part of real history today as it was the moment it happened. It is not a first-century attempt to portray the timelessness of a remarkable man thought to be in some sense divine.

Timothy's confidence in the theological truths he has learned is based upon two considerations:

First, Timothy *learned the tradition from those he could trust. Phillips* translates, "Remember from what sort of people your knowledge has come." These included not only Paul and other reliable witnesses but also Timothy's mother Eunice and his grandmother Lois (see 2 Tim. 1:5). He had not been taken in by smooth-talking charlatans but had learned the basics from reliable individuals whose lives measured up to the demands of the faith

Second, from earliest childhood Timothy *had been familiar with the "sacred writings"* (3:15, *RSV*). It is often noted that this expression *(hiera grammata)* occurs only here in the Bible (*graphē* is the normal word for Scripture). It refers to what we now call the Old Testament. Timothy had been nurtured as a child on the sacred Scripture of the Jewish faith. His reliance upon the written record of what God had done in history for the redemption of His chosen people was the normal response of a Jewish boy brought up in a God-fearing home.

Paul notes that these sacred writings are able to give a specific sort of wisdom. It is a wisdom that leads to salvation. They inform a person not only of God's power to save but of man's basic need for that salvation. Scriptural truth does not automatically result in salvation. It is *able* to lead a person to that end but it must be accompanied by "faith in Christ Jesus." The letter of the law is powerless. It achieves its end only when acted upon by faith.

The final two verses of chapter 3 (16,17) are regularly used to support the doctrine of the inspiration of Scripture. And so they do. In the immediate context, however, the emphasis is more on the usefulness of Scripture than upon its inspiration. The previous verse has just indicated that Scripture provides a "wisdom that leads to salvation" *(Williams)*. While this wisdom stems from the fact that it is "God-breathed," its usefulness is clearly indicated by its role in "teaching, rebuking, correcting and training in righteousness."

But let us look first at what the verse teaches about the inspiration of Scripture. Note first of all that "all Scripture" is inspired. In this context Scripture refers to the Old Testament. By logical extension we can rightfully include the New Testament, although this, of course, was not in Paul's mind at the moment. Elsewhere Paul taught that the apostolic message was not the word of men but "the word of God" (1 Thess. 2:13). But at the time when Paul wrote to Timothy the New Testament as we know it now had not yet been gathered into one book—in fact, much of it had not even been written (*e.g.*, some of the Gospels, the general Epistles, Revelation). By *all* Scripture Paul intends to emphasize that every separate part of it was useful in some way.

Scripture is "God-breathed." The word occurs nowhere else in the Bible. It means that Scripture is the product of God's creative breath. As God formed man from the dust of the ground and "breathed into his nostrils the breath of life" so that "man became a living being" (Gen. 2:7) so it is that God's breath has turned lifeless words on paper into a living utterance. Had God not breathed life into the words of the prophets they would have been no more than the words of men. As it is when we read the prophets we find ourselves confronted with God Himself who speaks to us directly through what was written by chosen men of old.

Because Scripture is God-breathed it is also of great profit. Its usefulness is seen in four areas: *teaching* (the basic source for instruction in Christian doctrine), *rebuking* (truth has a way of reminding man of his many imperfections), *correcting* (Scripture provides the norm by which we define and determine error), and *training in righteousness* (it lays out goals for man's moral development and tells him how to

144

discipline himself in order to reach these goals).

The ultimate purpose of Scripture is that "the man of God may be thoroughly equipped [proficient, well-prepared] for every good work." The salvation Paul speaks of in these verses is spiritual deliverance from a wasted life of self-centeredness. God wants to save us to a life of good works. Salvation is always *from* sin and its penalty but it is not simply *to* heaven and its rewards. It is *to* a life of good works (see Eph. 2:10; Titus 2:11-14). This truth needs to be learned by those who, while claiming membership in God's family, live as if pleasure in this life were the supreme good. Redeemed people are free to live in love, not free from its obligations.

That "all Scripture is God-breathed" (other translations have "divinely inspired," "God-inspired") is Scripture's most important statement about itself. We do not, however, accept it as inspired only on the basis of its own claim. We come to accept Scripture as the Word of God and therefore trustworthy on the basis of such criteria as fulfilled prophecy, the testimony of Jesus, consistency of doctrine, the witness of the Spirit. Once accepted we believe all of its doctrines; and its divine inspiration is one of these doctrines.

Since the Bible is divinely inspired what should be our personal relationship to it? Are God's words in print any less authoritative than His words when originally spoken? How can we help overcome the tendency to make inspiration a subject of theological debate rather than a truth for personal guidance? Is the Bible any less the Word of God because it comes through the words of men? From a theological standpoint is there any difference between literature which is "inspiring" and the Bible which is "inspired"?

10

SECOND TIMOTHY FOUR

A Final and Solemn Charge (4:1-5)

As Paul nears the end of his letter he lays upon Timothy a most serious and solemn charge (the Greek verb means "to declare solemnly and emphatically"). He knows that the time for his departure has come (see v. 6). Timothy will have to stand on his own from now on. He will have to bear the responsibilities of leadership and carry on where Paul will leave off. This calls for understanding and courage. It is essential that Timothy grasp the full significance of his crucial role in the life of the church.

The charge is made "in the presence of God and of Christ Jesus." Both God the Father and God the Son are summoned to witness the responsibility laid upon Timothy by Paul, that aged warrior of the gospel. Christ is portrayed as the One who is about to judge the living and the dead. Judgment is in His hands and He will determine how well Timothy carries out his charge. This judgment is to take place at Christ's appearing when He comes to establish His kingdom. All the phrases of verse 1 join to heighten the sense of urgency with which the apostolic charge is given.

The charge itself is straightforward and simple—"Preach the Word" (v. 2). The Greek verb means to herald or to proclaim. It has the idea of public proclamation of an important message. The noun form describes the individual who in classical times went throughout the city proclaiming in a loud voice the messages of the king. As a sort of town crier he played a crucial role in ancient days. His responsibility was to declare so all could hear exactly what the king wanted to be known. He must make known without alteration the message that had been delivered to him.

Timothy is God's "town crier." The message he proclaims is the Word—God's glad tidings that Jesus Christ, by His death and resurrection, has brought salvation to man. Timothy could undoubtedly have held the interest of large crowds by recounting his many exciting adventures on the road with the apostle Paul. His charge, however, was to preach the Word. If contemporary preaching needs any one thing more than anything else it is a return to biblical preaching. Today's heralds need to hear again Paul's solemn charge, "Preach the Word." Laymen are tired of oft-repeated illustrations and well-intentioned psychological tips under the guise of spiritual insight. They want to hear the Word. Amos predicted our day when he wrote:

> "Behold, the days are coming," says the Lord God, "when I will send a famine on the land; not a famine of bread, nor a thirst for water, but of hearing the words of the Lord." (Amos 8:11, *RSV*).

Timothy is to press home the message "on all occasions, convenient or inconvenient" (v. 2, *NEB*). The urgency of the message overrides whether or not the situation is entirely favorable. The gospel messenger makes a three-fold appeal to *reason* ("correct"), *conscience* ("rebuke") and *will* ("encourage"). He is to carry out his task, however, with "great patience and careful instruction." The ministry is no place for an individual with a short fuse. Correction and rebuke rarely accomplish their purpose first time around. In fact, people are so sensitive that it may take considerable time to regain balance after being confronted with the need for change. But in time God's Spirit reshapes the way believers live so that they begin to act in the way Christ would have responded under similar circumstances. Note as well the role of instruction (apostolic teaching) in the work of the ministry. The Word is also our guide for all correction, rebuke and encouragement.

Paul predicts a time when men won't put up with wholesome teaching (see v. 3). In contrast with false doctrine which undermines spiritual health, the gospel message restores spiritual wholeness. In place of sound doctrine men will search out teachers who will tell them what they want to hear. Their ears itch for some novel idea or new interpretation. It is not the truth that directs their thoughts but the lure of their own evil inclinations.

Popular leaders inevitably tell people what they want to hear. The prophet, God's spokesman, tells people what they need to know. Barclay reports that Alcibiades used to say to Socrates: "Socrates, I hate you, because every time I meet you, you make me see what I am."

By nature men avoid the truth (see v. 4). They prefer deception to reality. The gospel is a light which illumines the dark corners of men's lives. No wonder it is resisted. Men turn from the truth and embrace myth. The unreal world of fiction and fable provides men with places to hide. Since it recognizes no final truth it makes no judgments. Without judgment man is free to wander as he pleases. Only one problem exists—man is still accountable to a real God in a real world. By shutting one's eyes the light is never put out.

Over against all those who have turned aside, Timothy is to continue steadfast in his role as leader of the congregation (see v. 5). Four obligations are singled out:

First, Timothy is to *keep his head in all situations.* The word means to be sober or self-controlled. So often in human relations it is the unexpected that throws us off balance. Leadership calls for a level of maturity that can maintain composure under the most trying of times.

Second, Timothy is to *endure hardship.* Paul has just written that those who want to live godly lives in union with Christ Jesus will be persecuted (see 2 Tim. 3:12). The work of the ministry involves opposition, both from men and from the powers of the underworld. To be at ease in Zion is to be so ineffective that no opposition from Satan is called for. In the Sermon on the Mount Jesus warned, "Woe to you when all men speak well of you" (Luke 6:26).

Third, Timothy is to *do the work of an evangelist.* The evangel is the good news that God was in Christ reconciling the world to Himself (see 2 Cor. 5:19). Men everywhere need to hear that forgiveness is available. The role of the evangelist is to declare to all this good news.

Finally, in an all-inclusive clause, Timothy is exhorted to *"discharge all the duties of [his] ministry."* As *The Living Bible* has it, "Leave nothing undone that you ought to do." Timothy is to carry out his ministry to the full. No one or no responsibility is to

149

be neglected. Leadership demands complete dedication to the task.

Timothy is charged with the responsibility of correcting, rebuking, and encouraging the believers at Ephesus (see v. 2). The task is not unlike that of a parent. At times a parent must correct or reprove; at other times it is necessary to admonish or rebuke. More often than most of us expect it is appropriate to encourage. When to respond in a particular way is determined by the specific situation, the child under consideration, and the history of one's previous attempts to foster growth and development.

In your own experience which of the three methods listed above (correct, rebuke, encourage) is most frequently used by preachers? Which one is reflected by the statement "Don't preach at me!"? Why do you think that encouragement is so often missing in the average pulpit-pew relationship? How do you personally respond to spiritual encouragement? Is encouragement more effective for you than censure? Should the same emphasis of positive motivation be applied to the family? Why do you think that those who bear responsibility for the conduct of others are so often somewhat negative?

In Retrospect (4:6-8)

Paul fully realized that the end of his life and ministry was at hand. He writes, therefore, that he is "already being poured out like a drink offering." The background for the metaphor is the Jewish custom of pouring out an offering of wine at the foot of the altar (see Num. 28:7; Sirach 50:15, *Apoc.*). Paul views his coming martyrdom as a sacrifice to God. As such it will be pleasing and acceptable.

He writes that the time of his departure has come. The word literally is "unloosing." It describes the loosing of a ship from its moorings (thus *Montgom-*

ery's translation: "the time of my unmooring is at hand") or the loosing of ropes that support a tent. The picture is one of death as a release from all the restrictions imposed by life. Man is bound by his innate tendency to sin. Even though in Christ he receives a new nature the old man lingers on. It continually attempts to impede his progress toward spiritual maturity. The tension is mirrored in Paul's exclamation, "Who will rescue me from this body of death?" (Rom. 7:24). Departure from this life is a release from all that separates us from God. Primarily we will be loosed from our natural inclination to sin. As John says, "When he appears, we shall be like him" (1 John 3:2). It is death that provides the occasion for this marvelous transformation. No wonder death held no terror for the apostle.

As Paul looks back over his life he can report three major achievements:

First, "I have *fought the good fight*" (2 Tim. 4:7). It is an athletic contest, not warfare, that Paul has in mind. A literal translation would be, "I have struggled the good struggle" (the Greek noun, which appears in the cognate verb as well, is *agōn*; compare the English "agony"). One writer feels that the apostle may have had a wrestling match in mind. Note that it is the *contest* (not his involvement in it) which is called noble or good.

Second, "I have *finished the race.*" Again Paul draws his metaphor from the athletic games. His claim is not that he won the race but that he didn't give up. We have all watched a distance runner drop out of a race. Hopefully it is not because he has lagged behind and gotten so discouraged that he decided to quit. Neither on the track nor in the church is there any place for those who give up when the going gets tough. Paul faced great obstacles (read about them in

151

2 Cor. 11:23-28) but carried on through to the very end.

Third, "I have *kept the faith.*" Some think that the reference is to an athlete's pledge that he had kept all the rules that would qualify him for the Olympic games (*e.g.*, at least 10 months of intensive training). Thus Paul would be saying that in the great Christian contest he has conducted himself with honor. The statement should probably be taken in the wider sense of loyalty to his appointment as an apostle and herald of the gospel. At the end of his career he can look back and say that he has been true to Christ and the charge laid upon him.

As a result of his faithfulness he knows that there is laid in store for him "the crown of righteousness" (2 Tim. 4:8). The word for "crown" is regularly used to designate the laurel wreath awarded to the winners in the Olympic games (not the *diadēma* or royal crown of Persian origin). It is not a crown consisting of righteousness but a crown which is the reward for an upright life. Paul's laurel wreath is eternal life itself.

The crown is to be awarded by "the Lord, the righteous Judge." Athletic judges were fallible and at times partial. Not so with Christ. Or perhaps Paul was thinking of the judges who sat in Nero's court and would be passing verdict on his own case before long. The only really important verdict has to do with the quality of his spiritual ministry, and that will be given by the one Judge who is absolutely righteous. Unlike the awards given at the games, Paul's victory wreath awaits the day of Christ's "appearing." The word is rich in meaning and pictures the return of Christ as a royal visit by a reigning sovereign. The crown goes not only to Paul but to all "who have set their hearts on his coming appearance" *(NEB)*.

The New Testament church is a great multitude of loyal subjects who know beyond the shadow of a doubt that Jesus Christ is Lord of lords and King of kings and that the day of His universal recognition is just around the corner. They long for His manifestation. At His coronation evil will be forever destroyed and the coming glorious age of His visible and eternal reign will begin. Believers eagerly await this momentous day with breathless wonder.

I once heard a story about a journalist who was in charge of the obituaries. One morning when he had no death to record he idly put a sheet of blank paper in his typewriter and wrote his name at the top. He then found himself writing his own obituary:

> I have been a good husband and a fine father. I have contributed to a number of worthy causes. I have left a reputation of absolute integrity. My friends are many.

By the time he had finished the page he had already committed himself to the task of living up to his own obituary.

Paul approached the close of his life with satisfaction. He had finished the course and kept the faith. He knew that a crown of righteousness would be his.

Our lives are getting on. How are we doing? What sort of statements would you like to see in your obituary? Are you living each day with these major goals in mind? What sort of achievements are the only ones of any real value when viewed in the light of eternity? Can you think of ways to make these goals a stronger motivating force in your daily life?

Personal Notes (4:9-22)

In the final paragraphs of his last letter Paul mentions a number of individuals who would be known to Timothy. Overall the section has a rather somber tone. Paul has been left quite alone without the personal support and encouragement of other believers. "Only Luke is with [him]" (v. 11). He asks Timothy to do his best to come to Rome as soon as possible. Bring Mark (see v. 11) and pick up my cloak and scrolls on your way through Troas (see v. 13). No one stood by me at my preliminary trial (see v. 16), but God delivered me in that time of crisis (see v. 17). Try "to get here before winter," Timothy (v. 21). "Grace be with you" (v. 22).

Demas is mentioned in the letter to Philemon (along with Luke and certain others) as a "fellow worker" of Paul (Philem. 24; see Col. 4:14). The only other thing we know of him is supplied by the present verse—he deserted Paul and went to Thessalonica. The word means "to leave behind," that is, to forsake or abandon. It suggests that Demas withdrew whatever support he could have given at the very time Paul needed it. Perhaps in the preliminary trial Demas realized what it would cost him personally to stand by the apostle. He deserted Paul "because he loved this world." He had forgotten that Christ had died in order to "rescue us from the present evil age" (Gal. 1:4) and that "friendship with the world is hatred toward God" (Jas. 4:4). Some have wished to save Demas' reputation by identifying him with the Demetrius of 3 John 12 of whom it is written that he was "well spoken of by everyone." But Demas was a common name and no compelling reason exists to encourage this connection.

We know little of Crescens except that he went to Galatia presumably from Ephesus. There is no need to consider him to be a deserter like Demas. If Galatia here refers to ancient Gaul (eastern Europe) rather than the Roman province by that name (part of modern Turkey) we have an important witness to the westward expansion of the Christian church. Titus had apparently finished his work in Crete and had by this time gone on to Dalmatia (modern Yugoslavia).

Only Luke remains with Paul. In an earlier imprisonment he is referred to as "our dear friend Luke, the doctor" (Col. 4:14). Luke remains to the very end carrying on a ministry of personal care for the apostle in chains.

Timothy is instructed to pick up Mark along the way and bring him when he comes. It will be remembered that Mark was the young man who left Paul and Barnabas when, on the first missionary journey, they turned inland from Pamphylia and headed up into the dangerous central plateau of Asia Minor (see Acts 13:5,13). Differing opinions of Mark led to a separation between the two missionaries before the second journey (see Acts 15:36-41). It is good to learn that by the time of the first Roman imprisonment Mark is back in the apostle's circle of close associates (see Col. 4:10). Now Paul wants Mark perhaps because he would be useful in serving the apostle's personal needs. It is equally possible, however, that verse 11 means that Mark would be useful in helping Paul carry out the ministry of the gospel. In either case there is no commendation higher than to be judged useful in the work of the Lord. The major accomplishments in the forward progress of the faith rest upon the apparently ordinary and mundane activities of faithful believers.

Oh yes, adds Paul, "I sent Tychicus to Ephesus" (v. 12). Tychicus was a native of Asia Minor and a companion of Paul on his last journey to Jerusalem (see Acts 20:4). He is being sent to Ephesus probably to replace Timothy during the time the latter is in Rome with Paul.

That Timothy is to bring Paul's cloak and scrolls (see v. 13) from Troas doesn't necessarily indicate that the apostle was forgetful. The cloak was a large sleeveless garment made of heavy material. A hole in the middle was for the head. As winter came on it would offer some protection against the cold of a Roman prison. The scrolls would be rolls of papyrus (the most common writing material of antiquity) and the parchments were animal skins, more expensive but having the advantage of reuse. It has been suggested that Paul was asking for his private documents such as proof of citizenship. It is much more probable that the scrolls and parchments were copies of Scripture. They could have been written accounts of the teachings of Christ or Old Testament proof texts. In any case it was important to Paul at the close of his life to have them close at hand.

The next person mentioned is Alexander the coppersmith (or perhaps "metalworker" *[NIV]*, or "blacksmith" *[Moffatt]*). In Paul's first letter to Timothy he mentioned a certain Alexander who had been excommunicated from the church (see 1 Tim. 1:20). There is no way of knowing for sure whether these two references are to the same person. Probably not because the one had been removed from the congregation and the other is identified by his occupation (presumably to prevent confusion with some other person of the same name). The only other Alexander mentioned in the New Testament was the Jew who was shouted down in the public assembly at Ephesus when he tried to mount a defense for Paul (see Acts 19:33,34).

Alexander the metalworker "did [Paul] a great deal of harm." The verb literally means "to display" and was often used to describe activities of a legal informer. Some therefore think that Alexander may have been a renegade Christian who at Paul's preliminary trial brought false and evil accusations against him. Conybeare translates, "the brass-founder charged me with much evil in his declaration." This conjecture is strengthened by the fact that the verb tense in verse 15 ("He strongly opposed our message") suggests a specific act rather than continuing opposition.

In any case Paul does not take it upon himself to redress the wrong. "The Lord will repay him for what he has done" (v. 14). This does not reveal any desire for revenge on Paul's part: it is simply a prediction of what will happen. God is just and will not allow such a misrepresentation of truth to go scot-free. Timothy is warned to stay clear of Alexander. Be on guard because he is a strong adversary of our cause.

Paul's "first defense" (v. 16) was not a trial conducted during his first Roman imprisonment. It was rather the preliminary hearing during a second imprisonment which would lead to a later trial. At this first defense no one rallied to Paul's support. The verb used is a technical term for a witness speaking in behalf of a prisoner. It seems incredible that at Rome no one among the believers would take the stand in defense of Paul. Yet here we learn that such was the case. Paul was deserted, left in the lurch. How bitterly disappointing this must have been to the apostle who had poured out his life in the proclamation of the gospel and for those who would gladly receive its benefits. Yet his response is very much like that of his Master's, "May it not be held against them" (compare Luke 23:34, "Father, forgive them, for they do not know what they are doing"; also Stephen in Acts 7:60). To live in fellowship with Christ is to become like Him. An unchanged life denies the claim of a personal relationship.

While no one came to Paul's defense in his time of need, the Lord stood by him and provided strength. Even without supporting testimony the judge had decided to postpone any verdict until a later hearing. This was the Lord's doing, for Paul could easily have been pronounced guilty at the first trial. Paul's statement that through him the message was fully proclaimed so that all the Gentiles would hear (see v. 17) is a way of saying that the preliminary trial gave him the opportunity to explain his position to the strategically important Roman tribunal. Because the Lord enabled him he was "delivered from the lion's mouth," that is, he was saved from an immediate and adverse decision. Without God's intervention the tide of opinion would have gone against him and he would have been immediately executed.

This experience of deliverance leads Paul to affirm that the Lord will continue to deliver him from every evil attack (see v. 18) and bring him safely into the heavenly kingdom. Here Paul's thoughts shift from physical to spiritual deliverance. He knows that martyrdom is just around the corner (see vv. 6-8). Since the Lord has preserved him (physically) through all previous assaults, he is now confident that the Lord will deliver him (spiritually) in the last hour. Such confidence in God leads Paul to exclaim, "To him be glory for ever and ever. Amen." The apostle's ministry began with a divine mandate. It ends with a doxology.

Priscilla and her husband Aquila (she is named before him six times in the New Testament, perhaps because she was a more dominant personality) were two of Paul's most devoted helpers. Expelled from Rome by an imperial edict they worked with Paul in Corinth and then in Ephesus (see Acts 18:2,3,18,19,

158

26). Onesiphorus is discussed in the commentary on 2 Timothy 1:16,17. In Romans 16:23 Erastus is identified as "director of public works" in Corinth. Trophimus, a Gentile Christian and native of Ephesus (see Acts 21:29) was left ill at Miletus, a seacoast town near Ephesus.

There is a plaintive note in Paul's request that Timothy do his best to get to Rome "before winter" (v. 21). As the great missionary and apostle of the Christian faith approaches the end he is avoided or forgotten by most. He shares the loneliness of Christ. He wants Timothy his dear son to come to his side before the winter storms make it impossible for ships to sail from Ephesus to Rome.

We know little or nothing about the last four persons mentioned by Paul. All except Eubulus have Latin names which fact strengthens the position that 2 Timothy was written from Rome. It has been conjectured that Claudia was perhaps the wife of Pudens and mother of Linus. This Linus may have been the one who according to tradition became the bishop of Rome following the apostles Peter and Paul.

Paul closes his letter with a benediction. "The Lord be with your spirit. Grace be with you" (v. 22). How appropriate for the apostle of the grace of God to close his final letter on the subject of God's unmerited favor bestowed upon man. The pronoun "you" is plural indicating that although the letter is addressed to Timothy, it is intended for the entire congregation.

In the closing paragraphs of his letter Paul mentions 17 different individuals. To be sure, not all of them are commended. Yet all are called by name and treated as individuals. Paul's fame as the leading theologian-missionary of Western Christianity did not lead him into the error of considering people in the mass. It may well have been his life of intercessory prayer that helped him to think of people as separate and personal.

Since no one of us likes to be lumped together for the purpose of identification—"Meet a friend of my brother/ an acquaintance from Illinois/ a bassoon player in the orchestra"—why is it that we so easily forget names? When a person says that he can't remember names is he perhaps revealing the fact that he doesn't actually care enough about other people to bother with his name? Would it be possible to pray regularly for a person and not know his name? Do you pray for individuals or classes of people (the sick, the lonesome, the delinquent)? Should not concern for names on the part of Christians be more than a Dale Carnegie gimmick?